Southern Living®
ALL-TIME FAVORITE
30-MINUTE
MEALS

Southern Living®

ALL-TIME FAVORITE

30-MINUTE
MEALS

Compiled and Edited by
Jean Wickstrom Liles

Oxmoor House®

Library of Congress Catalog Number: 95-67710
ISBN: 0-8487-2221-3
Manufactured in the United States of America
First Printing 1995

Editor-in-Chief: Nancy J. Fitzpatrick
Editorial Director, Special Interest Publications: Ann H. Harvey
Senior Foods Editor: Susan Carlisle Payne
Senior Editor, Editorial Services: Olivia Kindig Wells
Art Director: James Boone

SouthernLiving® ALL-TIME FAVORITE 30-MINUTE MEALS

Menu and Recipe Consultant: Jean Wickstrom Liles
Assistant Editor: Kelly Hooper Troiano
Copy Editor: Jane Phares
Editorial Assistants: Keri Bradford, Julie A. Cole
Indexer: Mary Ann Laurens
Concept Designer: Melissa Jones Clark
Designer: Rita Yerby
Senior Photographers: Jim Bathie; Charles Walton IV, *Southern Living* magazine
Photographers: Ralph Anderson; Tina Evans, J. Savage Gibson, Sylvia Martin, *Southern Living* magazine
Senior Photo Stylist: Kay E. Clarke
Photo Stylists: Virginia R. Cravens; Leslie Byars, Ashley Johnson, *Southern Living* magazine
Production and Distribution Director: Phillip Lee
Production Manager: Gail Morris
Associate Production and Distribution Manager: John Charles Gardner
Associate Production Manager: Theresa L. Beste
Production Assistant: Marianne Jordan

Our appreciation to the editorial staff of *Southern Living* magazine for their contributions to this volume.

Cover: Festive Family Supper (menu on page 22)
Page 1: Quick-Fix Lunch (menu on page 73)
Page 2: Special Occasion Luncheon (menu on page 125)

Contents

Make It . . . Quick & Easy

Even with today's fast-paced schedules it's possible to have quick, easy, *and* delicious meals on the table in 30 minutes. Many of our recipes have a short ingredient list and may use quality convenience products in a unique way. These recipes, along with our TimeSaver tips, are designed for speed. While your hands-on preparation shouldn't exceed 30 minutes, note that most menus contain one or more make-ahead recipes. These are designated by the diamond symbol (◆) in the menu.

Organize Your Kitchen

Arrange food, equipment, and utensils in your pantry and cabinets for easy access and quick cooking.

• **Stock** your pantry with staple items. Group similar items together, and rotate older items to the front to use first. Keep as many labels as possible in plain sight for at-a-glance inventory.

• **Alphabetize** spices on a turntable or rack for speedy identification.

• **Use** plastic drawer dividers to organize kitchen drawers. Keep small measuring items together, and separate small utensils from large utensils.

• **Keep** knives sharpened and in a safe, convenient holder.

• **Keep** a cutting board on the counter near the sink to save food preparation time.

• **Store** aluminum foil, plastic wrap, and food storage bags in a drawer near your work area.

• **Use** decorative jars near the cooktop and mixing center to store the following items: wooden spoons, plastic scrapers, metal spatulas, tongs, whisks, long-handled cooking spoons and forks, kitchen shears, and a ladle.

• **Hang** pot holders next to the oven, cooktop, and microwave oven. Keep a trivet on the counter near the oven for hot containers.

• **Use** stackable canisters for flour, sugar, and coffee to save space. Keep a dry measuring cup in each canister to use as a handy scoop and measure.

Shortcut Strategies

Use these shortcuts to streamline your time.

• **Read** all the recipes in the menu and assemble all the ingredients and equipment.

• **Make** a game plan. First start with make-aheads; then plan the portion of the meal that involves more total time than active time—such as cooking the rice.

• **Plan** for leftovers by fixing a large quantity or simply doubling a recipe; freeze or refrigerate the remainder so you will have a heat-and-eat meal to serve another day.

• **Measure** dry ingredients before moist ones to minimize cleanup. Before measuring honey and other sticky ingredients, rinse the measure with hot water; then the honey will slide right out.

• **Chop** an ingredient only once, even if it's called for in two recipes in the menu. Divide the ingredients into appropriate portions.

• **Chop** dry ingredients such as breadcrumbs or nuts in a food processor first. Then chop or shred moist or wet foods without washing the workbowl.

• **Use** a food processor to chop, slice, or shred several ingredients consecutively or together without washing the workbowl if the ingredients will later be combined.

• **Chop** and freeze ½-cup portions of green pepper, onion, and parsley in zip-top freezer bags, or purchase prepackaged frozen chopped onion and green pepper. When you have extra time, prepare dry breadcrumbs, shredded cheese, and toasted nuts to freeze.

• **Buy** ingredients in closest-to-usable form. Choose such items as skinned and boned chicken breasts, peeled shrimp, and shredded cheese. Select bags of precut produce at your supermarket, or purchase ready-prepared ingredients at the salad bar.

• **When** slicing vegetables like carrots, green onions, or celery, slice 3 or 4 pieces at a time.

• **Cut** vegetables into small pieces or thin slices to cook faster.

• **To** peel a tomato or peach, dip the fruit into boiling water for 15 to 30 seconds; the skin will slip off easily.

• **Shape** patties for burgers in a flash. Shape ground meat into a log, partially freeze, and cut into slices of preferred thickness.

• **Buy** precut packaged meat for stir-frying. Or to slice your own, first partially freeze the meat; then slice it across the grain into thin strips.

• **Substitute** an equal amount of ready-to-serve chicken broth for homemade chicken stock.

• **Use** refrigerated or fresh pasta. It cooks faster than dried. Boil-in-bag rice takes half the time of regular rice to cook.

• **Cook** extra quantities of rice and pasta; freeze in individual or family-size portions up to 6 months. Microwave to thaw.

Make It . . . Quick and Easy   7

• **Add** pasta to boiling water in small batches. A few drops of oil added to the water prevents pasta from sticking together.

Put Equipment to Use

Utilize kitchen gadgets and equipment to maximize your time and trim minutes off daily meal preparations.

• **Use** two sets of measuring cups and spoons so you can measure consecutive ingredients without washing or wiping out the measure repeatedly.

• **Use** two cutting boards to hold separately chopped ingredients; this will keep you from having to transfer the items to another container.

• **Chop** canned tomatoes right in the can with kitchen shears.

• **Use** a salad spinner to rinse and dry vegetables.

• **Keep** a swivel-bladed vegetable peeler handy for tasks other than peeling vegetables. Use it to shred a small amount of cheese, remove strings from celery stalks, or make quick chocolate curls.

• **Use** a pastry blender to slice hard-cooked eggs and butter or

to mash avocados for chunky guacamole.

• **Use** nonstick cookware and bakeware for easy cleanup.

• **Place** a metal colander upside down over the skillet when frying or sautéing; this will prevent splatters while allowing steam to escape.

• **Use** a pizza cutter to cut dough or to cut day-old bread into cubes for croutons—it's faster than a knife.

• **When** baking or roasting, remember to preheat the oven before preparing the recipe; if you forget, it will take the oven about 20 minutes to reach the specified temperature.

• **Avoid** splatters with your electric mixer by punching holes in a paper plate; insert beaters, and keep the surface of the plate even with the top of the bowl.

• **Use** a meat mallet to tenderize and flatten meat.

• **Use** a microwave oven for thawing foods quickly or for shortcuts such as softening butter and melting chocolate.

• **To** make cracker crumbs or cookie crumbs without a food processor, place crackers or cookies in a heavy-duty, zip-top plastic bag; roll with a rolling pin or pound with a meat mallet.

Microwave Shortcuts Save Time

These techniques are quicker to do in the microwave than in the conventional oven and yield good results.

COOKING BACON—Cook at HIGH

1 slice	1 to 2 minutes
4 slices	3½ to 4½ minutes
6 slices	5 to 7 minutes

Place bacon on a microwave-safe rack in a 12- x 8- x 2-inch baking dish; cover with paper towels. Microwave at HIGH until bacon is crisp. Drain bacon.

MELTING BUTTER OR MARGARINE—Cook at HIGH

1 to 2 tablespoons	35 to 45 seconds
¼ to ½ cup	1 minute
¾ cup	1 to 1½ minutes
1 cup	1½ to 2 minutes

Place butter in a microwave-safe glass measure; microwave at HIGH until melted.

SOFTENING BUTTER OR MARGARINE—Cook at LOW (10% power)

1 to 2 tablespoons	15 to 30 seconds
¼ to ½ cup	1 to 1¼ minutes
1 cup	1½ to 1¾ minutes

Place butter in a microwave-safe measure or plate; microwave at LOW until softened.

MELTING CHOCOLATE—Cook at MEDIUM (50% power)

1 to 2 squares	1½ to 2 minutes
4 to 5 squares	2 to 2½ minutes
½ to 1 cup morsels	2 to 3 minutes
1½ cups morsels	3 to 3½ minutes

Place chocolate in a small bowl; microwave at MEDIUM until melted, stirring once.

TOASTING NUTS—Cook at HIGH

¼ cup chopped nuts	3 minutes
½ cup chopped nuts	3½ minutes
1 cup chopped nuts	4 to 5 minutes

Spread nuts on a pieplate. Microwave at HIGH until toasted; stir at 2-minute intervals.

MICRO-BAKED POTATOES—Cook at HIGH

1 medium (6 to 7 ounces)	4 to 6 minutes
2 medium	7 to 8 minutes
4 medium	12 to 14 minutes

Rinse potatoes; prick several times with a fork. Arrange potatoes at least 1 inch apart. (If more than 2 potatoes, arrange them in a circle.) Microwave at HIGH until done, turning and rearranging potatoes once. Let stand 5 minutes before serving.

Handy Substitutions

Needed Ingredient	Substitute
Baking Products:	
1 cup self-rising flour	1 cup all-purpose flour, 1 teaspoon baking powder, plus ½ teaspoon salt
1 cup cake flour	1 cup sifted all-purpose flour minus 2 tablespoons
1 cup all-purpose flour	1 cup cake flour plus 2 tablespoons
1 cup powdered sugar	1 cup sugar plus 1 tablespoon cornstarch (processed in food processor)
1 cup honey	1¼ cups sugar plus ¼ cup water
1 cup light corn syrup	1 cup sugar plus ¼ cup water
1 teaspoon baking powder	¼ teaspoon baking soda plus ½ teaspoon cream of tartar
1 tablespoon cornstarch (for thickening)	2 tablespoons all-purpose flour
1 tablespoon tapioca	1½ tablespoons all-purpose flour
1 (1-ounce) square unsweetened chocolate	3 tablespoons cocoa plus 1 tablespoon butter or margarine
Dairy Products:	
2 large eggs	3 small eggs
1 cup milk	½ cup evaporated milk plus ½ cup water
1 cup whipping cream	¾ cup milk plus ⅓ cup melted butter (for baking only; will not whip)
1 cup plain yogurt	1 cup buttermilk
1 cup sour cream	1 cup yogurt plus 3 tablespoons melted butter or 1 cup yogurt plus 1 tablespoon cornstarch
Vegetable Products:	
1 pound fresh mushrooms, sliced	1 (8-ounce) can sliced mushrooms, drained, or 3 ounces dried
1 medium onion, chopped	1 tablespoon instant minced onion or 1 tablespoon onion powder
3 tablespoons chopped sweet red or green pepper	1 tablespoon dried pepper flakes or 2 tablespoons chopped pimiento
3 tablespoons chopped shallots	2 tablespoons chopped onion plus 1 tablespoon chopped garlic
Seasoning Products:	
1 tablespoon chopped fresh herbs	1 teaspoon dried herbs or ¼ teaspoon powdered herbs
1 clove garlic	⅛ teaspoon garlic powder or ⅛ teaspoon minced dried garlic
1 tablespoon chopped chives	1 tablespoon chopped green onion tops
1 tablespoon grated fresh gingerroot or candied ginger	⅛ teaspoon ground ginger
1 tablespoon grated fresh horseradish	2 tablespoons prepared horseradish
1 tablespoon dried orange peel	1½ teaspoons orange extract or 1 tablespoon grated orange rind
1 (1-inch) vanilla bean	1 teaspoon vanilla extract
1 teaspoon garlic salt	⅛ teaspoon garlic powder plus ⅞ teaspoon salt
1 teaspoon ground allspice	½ teaspoon ground cinnamon plus ½ teaspoon ground cloves
1 teaspoon apple pie spice	½ teaspoon ground cinnamon, ¼ teaspoon ground nutmeg, ⅛ teaspoon ground cardamom
1 teaspoon pumpkin pie spice	½ teaspoon ground cinnamon, ¼ teaspoon ground ginger, ⅛ teaspoon ground allspice, ⅛ teaspoon ground nutmeg
Miscellaneous Products:	
¼ cup Marsala	¼ cup dry white wine plus 1 teaspoon brandy
1 tablespoon brandy	¼ teaspoon brandy extract plus 1 tablespoon water
½ cup balsamic vinegar	½ cup red wine vinegar (slight flavor difference)
1 cup tomato juice	½ cup tomato sauce plus ½ cup water
2 cups tomato sauce	¾ cup tomato paste plus 1 cup water
1 cup tomato sauce	⅜ cup tomato paste plus ½ cup water

What's for Supper?

Some nights supper has to be ready fast. These quick-fix recipes call for only a few ingredients and will help you get food on the table in a flash.

Soft Beef Tacos, Grilled Chicken, Golden Chops with Vegetables

Boiled Shrimp with Zippy Red Sauce, Sweet-and-Sour Chicken Nuggets, Sautéed Peppers

Oven-Fried Chicken Chimichangas, Broccoli-Shrimp Stuffed Potatoes, Pasta Salad

Caesar's Fish, Pecan-Crusted Turkey Cutlets, Sweet-and Sour Shrimp

Beef with Red Wine Marinade (page 14)

Soft Beef Tacos

Supper Olé

Soft Beef Tacos

1 pound ground beef
1 small onion, minced
2 cloves garlic, minced
½ green pepper, chopped
1 jalapeño pepper, seeded and minced
1 cup water
1 teaspoon ground cumin
1 teaspoon chili powder
½ teaspoon dried oregano
¼ teaspoon salt
⅛ teaspoon pepper
8 (7-inch) flour tortillas
2 cups shredded lettuce
2 tomatoes, chopped
1 cup (4 ounces) shredded Cheddar cheese
1 (8-ounce) carton guacamole
Commercial taco or picante sauce

Cook first 5 ingredients in a large skillet until meat is browned, stirring to crumble; drain well. Stir in water and next 5 ingredients; bring to a boil. Cover, reduce heat, and simmer over low heat 20 minutes, stirring occasionally. Uncover and cook 5 minutes.

Wrap tortillas securely in aluminum foil; bake at 350° for 10 minutes or until thoroughly heated.

Spoon equal amounts of meat mixture lengthwise down center of each tortilla. Top with lettuce, tomato, cheese, guacamole, and desired amount of taco sauce. Fold bottom third of tortillas over filling. Fold sides of tortillas in toward center, leaving top open. Secure with wooden picks, if necessary. Serve with additional taco sauce, if desired. **Yield: 4 servings.**

Cantaloupe Salad

½ cup mayonnaise
3 tablespoons frozen orange juice concentrate, thawed and undiluted
1 small cantaloupe, chilled
Leaf lettuce
1⅓ cups seedless green grapes, divided

Combine mayonnaise and orange juice concentrate, mixing well; set aside.

Cut cantaloupe into 4 sections; remove seeds, and peel. Place cantaloupe sections on lettuce leaves; spoon ⅓ cup grapes over and around each section. Drizzle with mayonnaise mixture. **Yield: 4 servings.**

Chocolate Cream Cheese Pie

1 (8-ounce) package cream cheese, softened
¾ cup sifted powdered sugar
¼ cup cocoa
1 (8-ounce) carton frozen whipped topping, thawed
1 (6-ounce) chocolate-flavored crumb crust
½ cup coarsely chopped pecans

Combine first 3 ingredients in a mixing bowl; beat at medium speed of an electric mixer until soft and creamy. Add whipped topping, folding until smooth. Spread over crumb crust, and sprinkle with pecans. Chill at least 4 hours. **Yield: one 9-inch pie.**

Sunset Supper
(pictured on page 11)
SERVES 6
◆ Beef with Red Wine Marinade • Leafy green salad • Tomato wedges
Parslied Garlic Bread • ◆ No-Bake Banana Pudding

Beef with Red Wine Marinade

1 (1½-pound) top round steak or flank steak
1 cup red wine
¼ cup soy sauce
¼ cup vegetable oil
1 teaspoon seasoned salt
1 teaspoon pepper
1 teaspoon dried oregano
1 teaspoon garlic juice

Place steak in a heavy-duty, zip-top plastic bag. Combine wine and remaining ingredients in a 2-cup glass measuring cup; stir well. Pour marinade over steak. Seal and chill 8 hours, turning occasionally.

Remove steak from marinade; grill, covered with grill lid, over medium coals (300° to 350°) 7 to 9 minutes on each side or to desired degree of doneness. To serve, slice steak across grain into thin slices. **Yield: 6 servings.**

Parslied Garlic Bread

1 (16-ounce) loaf French bread
¼ cup butter or margarine, softened
1 clove garlic, crushed
¼ cup chopped fresh parsley

Cut bread into 1-inch slices, cutting to, but not through, bottom crust. Combine butter, garlic, and parsley; spread between slices and on top of bread. Wrap in heavy-duty aluminum foil.

Grill bread over medium coals (300° to 350°), turning frequently, 10 to 15 minutes or until thoroughly heated. **Yield: 8 servings.**

No-Bake Banana Pudding

2 (3.4-ounce) packages vanilla instant
    pudding mix
1 (8-ounce) carton sour cream
3½ cups milk
Vanilla wafers
3 large bananas
1 (8-ounce) carton frozen whipped topping,
    thawed

Combine first 3 ingredients in a large bowl; beat at low speed of an electric mixer 2 minutes or until thickened.

Line bottom and sides of a 3-quart bowl with vanilla wafers. Slice 1 banana, and layer over wafers. Spoon one-third of pudding mixture over banana. Repeat layers two more times. Cover and chill. Spread whipped topping over pudding just before serving. **Yield: 10 servings.**

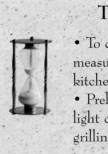

TimeSavers

• To chop parsley, place in a glass measuring cup and snip with kitchen shears.
• Preheat gas grill 20 minutes or light charcoal 30 minutes before grilling beef and bread.

South of the Border

Oven-Fried Chicken Chimichangas • Sunny Fruit Salad • Orange sherbet

Oven-Fried Chicken Chimichangas

3 (5-ounce) cans white chicken, drained and
    flaked
1 (4.5-ounce) can chopped green chiles,
    drained
1 cup (4 ounces) shredded Monterey Jack
    cheese
½ cup sliced green onions
8 (9-inch) flour tortillas
Vegetable oil
Shredded lettuce, salsa or picante sauce,
    sour cream

    Combine first 4 ingredients; set aside. Wrap
tortillas in damp paper towels; microwave at
HIGH 15 seconds or until hot. Brush both sides
of tortillas, one at a time, with vegetable oil (keep
remaining tortillas warm).
    Place a scant ½ cup chicken mixture just
below center of each tortilla. Fold in left and right
sides of tortilla to partially enclose filling. Fold up
bottom edge of tortilla; fold into a rectangle, and
secure with a wooden pick. Repeat with remaining tortillas and chicken mixture.
    Place filled tortillas on a lightly greased baking
sheet. Bake at 425° for 10 minutes or until crisp
and lightly browned. Serve with shredded lettuce,
salsa, and sour cream. **Yield: 4 servings.**

Oven-Fried Chicken Chimichangas

Sunny Fruit Salad

½ cup plain yogurt
2 tablespoons honey
1 teaspoon lemon juice
Pinch of grated nutmeg
1 cup orange sections
2 large bananas, peeled and cut into ½-inch
    slices
3 kiwifruit, peeled and cut into ½-inch slices
Lettuce leaves

    Combine first 4 ingredients in a medium
bowl. Add fruit, and toss gently. Serve on lettuce
leaves. **Yield: 4 servings.**

Sweet-and-Sour Special

SERVES 4

Sweet-and-Sour Chicken Nuggets • ◆ Cranberry Oriental • Sesame Bread Twists
Fortune cookies

Sweet-and-Sour Chicken Nuggets

1 (12-ounce) package frozen breaded chicken
   nuggets
1 cup water
1 cup uncooked instant rice
1 (16-ounce) can apricot halves, drained
1 (6-ounce) package frozen snow pea pods
¾ cup commercial sweet-and-sour sauce

Cook chicken according to package directions.
Set aside.

Bring water to a boil in a small saucepan; add
rice. Cover and remove from heat. Let rice stand
5 minutes.

Combine apricot halves, snow peas, and
sweet-and-sour sauce in a medium saucepan;
cook over medium heat until thoroughly heated.
Stir in chicken nuggets. Spoon rice onto a serving
plate, and arrange chicken mixture evenly over
rice. **Yield: 4 servings.**

Cranberry Oriental

1 (16-ounce) can whole-berry cranberry sauce
1 (8-ounce) can crushed pineapple, drained
1 teaspoon lemon juice
1 (8-ounce) carton sour cream
Lettuce leaves

Combine first 4 ingredients; stir until blended.
Pour mixture into an 8½- x 4½- x 3-inch loaf-
pan, and freeze until firm. Cut into 1-inch slices.
Serve on lettuce leaves. **Yield: 8 servings.**

Sesame Bread Twists

1 (8-ounce) can refrigerator crescent
   dinner rolls
1 large egg
⅓ cup sesame seeds

Unroll dough, and separate into 4 rectangles.
Press 2 rectangles together end to end, making 1
long rectangle. Cut each long rectangle lengthwise into 6 strips.

Beat egg lightly with a fork in a pieplate; set
aside. Sprinkle sesame seeds onto a 15- x 12-
inch piece of wax paper. Twist each strip of
dough several times; dip in egg, and roll in
sesame seeds.

Place strips 1 inch apart on a greased baking
sheet. Bake at 400° for 8 to 10 minutes or until
golden brown. **Yield: 1 dozen.**

TimeSavers

• Use leftover rice or prepare instant
or quick-cooking rice to serve with
chicken nuggets. One cup uncooked
instant rice equals 2 cups cooked.
• Make Cranberry Oriental ahead
and freeze in a loafpan or as individual salads in paper-lined muffin
pans. When frozen, transfer salads
to a freezer bag to use as needed.

Sweet-and-Sour Chicken Nuggets

Grilled Chicken

Grill-a-Meal

SERVES 4

Grilled Chicken • Lemony Corn on the Cob • Grilled Zucchini Fans
Sliced tomatoes • French bread • Pound Cake with Strawberry-Banana Topping

Grilled Chicken

½ cup white vinegar
½ cup balsamic vinegar
½ cup water
1 teaspoon chili powder
½ teaspoon dried oregano
½ teaspoon freshly ground black pepper
1 bay leaf
4 skinned and boned chicken breast halves

Combine first 7 ingredients in a heavy-duty, zip-top plastic bag. Add chicken, and marinate 20 minutes in refrigerator; remove chicken from marinade, reserving marinade. Bring marinade to a boil; discard bay leaf.

Grill chicken, covered with grill lid, over medium coals (300° to 350°) 6 minutes on each side, basting twice with marinade. **Yield: 4 servings.**

Lemony Corn on the Cob

¼ cup butter or margarine, softened
½ to 1 teaspoon lemon-pepper seasoning
4 ears fresh corn

Combine butter and lemon-pepper seasoning; spread on corn, and place each ear on a piece of heavy-duty aluminum foil. Roll foil lengthwise around each ear, and twist foil at each end.

Grill corn, covered with grill lid, over medium coals (300° to 350°) 20 minutes, turning after 10 minutes. **Yield: 4 servings.**

Grilled Zucchini Fans

3 tablespoons olive oil
¼ teaspoon garlic powder
4 small zucchini, cut into fans

Combine olive oil and garlic powder. Cut each zucchini into lengthwise slices, leaving slices attached on stem end. Fan slices out, and place on grill; brush zucchini with olive oil mixture.

Grill zucchini, covered with grill lid, over medium coals (300° to 350°) 5 minutes on each side, basting once with olive oil mixture. **Yield: 4 servings.**

Pound Cake with Strawberry-Banana Topping

2 tablespoons butter or margarine
2 tablespoons brown sugar
2 tablespoons lemon juice
¼ cup light rum
3 medium bananas, sliced
6 fresh strawberries, cut in half
Commercial pound cake

Melt butter in a skillet on grill. Add sugar, lemon juice, and rum; stir well. Cook, stirring constantly, until sugar dissolves (2 to 3 minutes). Add bananas and strawberries, and cook until bananas are soft but not mushy (about 2 minutes). Serve over pound cake. **Yield: 4 servings.**

Note: Strawberry-Banana Topping may be served over vanilla ice cream.

Special-Occasion Dinner

SERVES 4

Pecan-Crusted Turkey Cutlets • Quick-cooking rice mix • Sautéed Peppers
◆ Microwave Chocolate Pie • White wine

Pecan-Crusted Turkey Cutlets

¾ cup dry breadcrumbs
½ cup finely chopped pecans
½ teaspoon dried sage
¼ teaspoon salt
¼ teaspoon pepper
1 egg white, lightly beaten
1 tablespoon water
4 (4-ounce) turkey breast cutlets
Butter-flavored cooking spray

Combine first 5 ingredients in a shallow dish; set aside.

Combine egg white and water. Dip turkey cutlets in egg mixture; coat with breadcrumb mixture. Place on a baking sheet coated with cooking spray. Coat cutlets with cooking spray.

Bake at 350° for 12 minutes or until juices run clear when cut with a knife. **Yield: 4 servings.**

TimeSavers

• For packaged rice mixes, choose from long grain and wild rice, brown rice, and regular rice mixtures.
• Buy sliced peppers at a salad bar for Sautéed Peppers. Red, yellow, and green peppers make it a colorful dish, but you can use one or any combination of peppers.
• Prepare pie ahead. To save time, substitute 2 cups frozen whipped topping, thawed, for whipped cream.

Sautéed Peppers

1 yellow pepper, seeded and cut into thin strips
1 red pepper, seeded and cut into thin strips
1½ tablespoons olive oil
2 teaspoons balsamic or red wine vinegar
⅛ teaspoon garlic salt
1 teaspoon parsley flakes

Cook peppers in hot oil in a large skillet over high heat, stirring often, 6 minutes or until edges of peppers are lightly browned.

Reduce heat to medium; stir in vinegar, garlic salt, and parsley flakes. Cook 3 minutes, stirring often.

Serve immediately. **Yield: 4 servings.**

Microwave Chocolate Pie

2 cups miniature marshmallows
1 cup milk chocolate morsels
1 cup milk
1 (1-ounce) square unsweetened chocolate
1 cup whipping cream, whipped
1 (6-ounce) chocolate-flavored crumb crust

Combine first 4 ingredients in a 2-quart glass mixing bowl. Microwave at HIGH 4 to 5 minutes, stirring once. Cool.

Fold in whipped cream, and pour mixture into chocolate crust. Freeze until firm. **Yield: one (9-inch) pie.**

Pecan-Crusted Turkey Cutlets

Festive Family Supper
(pictured on cover)
SERVES 6
◆ Grilled Marinated Pork Tenderloin • Julienne Squash • French bread
Fudge Pie • Iced tea

Grilled Marinated Pork Tenderloin

2 (¾-pound) pork tenderloins
1 (8-ounce) bottle Italian salad dressing
Garnishes: cherry tomato halves, fresh parsley
    sprigs

Place pork tenderloins in a heavy-duty, zip-top plastic bag. Pour dressing over tenderloins; seal and chill 8 hours.

Remove tenderloins from marinade. Insert meat thermometer into tenderloins, being careful not to touch fat. Grill tenderloins, covered with grill lid, over medium-hot coals (350° to 400°) 12 to 15 minutes or until thermometer registers 160°, turning them once. Garnish, if desired. **Yield: 6 servings.**

Julienne Squash

1½ tablespoons vegetable oil
1½ tablespoons lemon juice
1½ tablespoons white vinegar
1 teaspoon salt-free herb-and-spice blend
⅛ teaspoon garlic salt
2 yellow squash
2 large zucchini

Combine first 5 ingredients. Stir well; set aside.
Cut yellow squash and zucchini into very thin strips. Arrange on a steaming rack, and place over boiling water; cover and steam 4 minutes.
Place vegetables in a bowl. Pour sauce over vegetables; toss gently to coat. **Yield: 6 servings.**

Fudge Pie

1 cup sugar
¼ cup all-purpose flour
¼ cup cocoa
½ cup butter or margarine, melted
2 large eggs, beaten
¼ teaspoon vanilla extract
½ cup chopped pecans
1 unbaked 9-inch pastry shell
Ice cream (optional)

Combine first 6 ingredients; stir well. Stir in pecans. Pour mixture into pastry shell. Bake at 350° for 25 minutes or until a wooden pick inserted in center comes out clean. Serve with ice cream, if desired. **Yield: one 9-inch pie.**

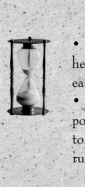

TimeSavers

• Marinate pork tenderloins in a heavy-duty, zip-top plastic bag for easy clean-up.
• Use a meat thermometer to test pork's doneness. Cutting the meat to see if it's still pink lets the juices run out.

A Family Affair

Golden Chops with Vegetables

6 (½-inch-thick) pork chops (about 2¼
   pounds)
1 (10¾-ounce) can golden mushroom soup,
   undiluted
¼ cup water
½ teaspoon rubbed sage
1 cup sliced carrot
½ cup chopped onion
1 medium-size green pepper, cut into strips

Brown pork chops in a large nonstick skillet;
remove pork chops and drain. Combine soup,
water, and sage in skillet; add carrot and onion.

Arrange pork chops over soup mixture; cover
and simmer over medium heat 15 minutes, stirring and rearranging pork chops once. Add green
pepper; cover and cook 10 additional minutes.
Yield: 6 servings.

Golden Chops with Vegetables

Soufflé Potatoes

2⅔ cups mashed potato mix
1 large egg, beaten
1 (2.8-ounce) can French-fried onions
¼ teaspoon salt
½ cup (2 ounces) shredded Cheddar cheese

Prepare mashed potato mix according to
package directions. Add egg, onions, and salt,
stirring until blended.

Spoon mixture into a greased 2-quart baking
dish; sprinkle with cheese. Bake, uncovered, at
350° for 5 minutes. **Yield: 6 to 8 servings.**

Quick Fruit Cobbler

1 (21-ounce) can cherry or blueberry pie filling
1 (8-ounce) can unsweetened crushed
   pineapple, drained
1 (9-ounce) package yellow cake mix
⅓ cup butter or margarine, melted

Spoon pie filling into a lightly greased 8-inch
square baking dish. Spoon pineapple over pie filling.

Sprinkle cake mix evenly over pineapple.
Drizzle butter over cake mix. Bake at 425° for 20
to 22 minutes. **Yield: 6 to 8 servings.**

Breaded Grouper Fillets

Just for Two

SERVES 2

Breaded Grouper Fillets • Green Beans with Mushrooms
Deli coleslaw in pepper cups • Chocolate Mint Sundaes

Breaded Grouper Fillets

½ cup nutlike cereal nuggets
2 tablespoons chopped fresh parsley
½ teaspoon dried rosemary
¼ teaspoon salt
2 (4-ounce) grouper fillets
⅓ cup low-fat plain yogurt
Garnish: lemon slices

Combine first 4 ingredients in a shallow dish; mix well. Brush fillets with yogurt on all sides; coat with cereal mixture. Place fillets in a 9-inch pieplate.

Microwave fillets at HIGH 1½ minutes; give dish a half-turn. Microwave 1½ to 2 minutes or until fish flakes easily when tested with a fork. Let stand 5 minutes. Garnish, if desired. **Yield: 2 servings.**

TimeSavers

• Chop parsley all at once for grouper and green beans.
• Buy the coleslaw at the deli to get a headstart on this menu. If fresh tomatoes are available, serve slaw in tomato cups rather than pepper cups.

Green Beans with Mushrooms

1 tablespoon minced onion
1 tablespoon vegetable oil
1 (8-ounce) can cut green beans, drained
1 tablespoon diced pimiento
1 teaspoon chopped fresh parsley
1 (4-ounce) can sliced mushrooms, drained
⅛ teaspoon salt
⅛ teaspoon pepper

Cook onion in hot oil in a medium skillet until transparent. Stir in beans and remaining ingredients; cover and cook over medium heat 10 minutes or until thoroughly heated. **Yield: 2 servings.**

Chocolate-Mint Sundaes

6 chocolate-covered mint patties
1 tablespoon milk
Vanilla ice cream

Combine mint patties and milk in a 1-cup glass measure. Cover with heavy-duty plastic wrap, and microwave at MEDIUM (50% power) 45 seconds or until patties melt. Serve warm over ice cream. **Yield: 2 servings.**

Catch-of-the-Day

SERVES 4

Caesar's Fish • Quick Potatoes • Tossed salad
Pineapple Soda

Caesar's Fish

Quick Potatoes

1 tablespoon olive oil
1 large onion, chopped
2 cloves garlic, minced
½ cup chopped sweet red pepper
½ teaspoon salt
¼ teaspoon pepper
¼ teaspoon hot sauce
3 cups unpeeled cubed potato
2 tablespoons butter or margarine

Heat olive oil in a 10-inch cast-iron skillet.
Add onion and garlic; cook over medium heat,
stirring constantly, until tender. Stir in red pepper
and next 3 ingredients; cook 2 minutes, stirring
constantly. Add potato and butter, stirring well.
Bake in skillet at 400° for 20 to 30 minutes.
Yield: 4 servings.

Caesar's Fish

1 pound flounder fillets
½ cup golden Caesar salad dressing
1 cup round buttery cracker crumbs
½ cup (2 ounces) shredded Cheddar cheese

Arrange fillets in a single layer in a lightly
greased 13- x 9- x 2-inch baking dish. Drizzle
Caesar dressing over fillets; sprinkle cracker
crumbs over top of fillets.
Bake fillets at 400° for 10 minutes; top with
cheese, and bake 5 additional minutes or until
fish flakes easily when tested with a fork. **Yield:
4 servings.**

Pineapple Soda

1 (8-ounce) can unsweetened crushed
    pineapple, undrained
2 tablespoons milk
1 pint vanilla ice cream
1 cup club soda

Combine first 3 ingredients in container of an
electric blender; blend until smooth. Stir in club
soda. Serve immediately. **Yield: 3½ cups.**

Shortcut Supper

Broccoli-Shrimp Stuffed Potatoes • Layered Fruit Salad
Pita Crisps • Commercial cookies

Broccoli-Shrimp Stuffed Potatoes

2 large baking potatoes (about 1¼ pounds)
⅓ cup loaf process cheese spread
2 tablespoons milk
1 cup fresh broccoli flowerets
1 (6-ounce) can shrimp, drained and rinsed
1 green onion, chopped

Scrub potatoes; prick several times with a fork. Place potatoes 1 inch apart on a microwave-safe rack or paper towel.

Microwave potatoes at HIGH 10 to 13 minutes, turning and rearranging once; let stand 2 minutes. Cut an X to within ½ inch of bottom of each potato. Squeeze potatoes from opposite sides and opposite ends to open; fluff with a fork.

Combine cheese spread and milk in a heavy saucepan; cook over low heat until cheese melts, stirring often. Remove from heat, and set aside.

Place broccoli in a 9-inch pieplate; cover and microwave at HIGH 2 to 3 minutes or until tender. Arrange broccoli and shrimp in potatoes. Spoon cheese sauce over potatoes, and sprinkle with green onions. **Yield: 2 servings.**

Broccoli-Shrimp Stuffed Potatoes

one-fourth of sour cream. Top with half of pineapple and one-fourth of sour cream. Repeat procedure with remaining ingredients. **Yield: 2 servings.**

Layered Fruit Salad

½ cup sliced strawberries
¼ cup sliced banana
¼ cup sour cream
½ cup pineapple chunks

Layer half each of strawberries and banana in a small serving dish; lightly spread fruit with

Pita Crisps

1 (6-inch) whole wheat pita bread round
1 tablespoon butter or margarine, melted

Split pita round to yield 2 flat discs. Cut each disc into 4 triangles; brush each triangle with melted butter.

Place triangles on paper towels in microwave. Microwave at HIGH 20 seconds or until edges curl.

Let stand to cool. **Yield: 2 servings.**

Family-Pleasing Shrimp

SERVES 4

Sweet-and-Sour Shrimp • Mandarin Orange-Lettuce Salad • ◆ Pineapple Pie

Sweet-and-Sour Shrimp

1 tablespoon vegetable oil
¼ cup chopped sweet red pepper
¼ cup sliced green onions
1 clove garlic, minced
1 pound peeled, medium-size fresh shrimp
⅓ cup red plum jam
2 tablespoons dry white wine
2 tablespoons white vinegar
2 tablespoons cocktail sauce
2 tablespoons chutney
½ teaspoon salt
¼ teaspoon dried crushed red pepper
¼ pound fresh snow pea pods
Hot cooked rice

Combine first 4 ingredients in a 1½-quart baking dish. Microwave at HIGH, uncovered, 2 to 3 minutes or until vegetables are tender; stir mixture at 1-minute intervals.

Add shrimp, and cover with heavy-duty plastic wrap; fold back a small edge of wrap to allow steam to escape. Microwave at MEDIUM (50% power) 8 to 10 minutes or until shrimp are opaque and firm, stirring at 3-minute intervals. Drain.

Combine jam and next 6 ingredients; stir well. Pour over shrimp, and stir gently. Cover and microwave at HIGH 1 to 1½ minutes or until sauce is heated. Add snow peas, and stir gently. Cover and microwave at HIGH 2 to 2½ minutes or until snow peas are crisp-tender. Let stand, covered, 1 to 2 minutes. Serve over cooked rice. **Yield: 4 servings.**

Mandarin Orange-Lettuce Salad

1 (16-ounce) package mixed lettuces
1 (11-ounce) can mandarin oranges, chilled and drained
⅓ cup golden raisins
1 (2-ounce) package cashew nuts, toasted (⅓ cup)
½ cup commercial Italian or sweet-and-sour salad dressing

Combine first 4 ingredients in a large bowl. Just before serving, pour dressing over salad and toss. **Yield: 4 servings.**

Pineapple Pie

1 (14-ounce) can sweetened condensed milk
½ cup lemon juice
1 (20-ounce) can crushed pineapple, drained
1 (8-ounce) carton frozen whipped topping, thawed
1 (9-ounce) graham cracker crust

Combine condensed milk and lemon juice; stir well. Fold in pineapple and whipped topping. Spoon mixture into crust. Chill. **Yield: one 9-inch pie.**

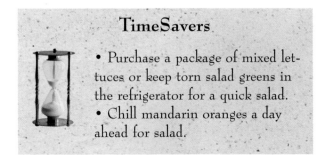

TimeSavers

• Purchase a package of mixed lettuces or keep torn salad greens in the refrigerator for a quick salad.
• Chill mandarin oranges a day ahead for salad.

Sweet-and-Sour Shrimp

Shrimp Boat Feast

SERVES 6

◆ Boiled Shrimp with Zippy Red Sauce • Pasta Salad
Onion-Cheese French Bread • Fresh fruit

Boiled Shrimp with Zippy Red Sauce

Pasta Salad

4 **cups uncooked rotini**
1 **medium zucchini, sliced**
2 **carrots, peeled and sliced**
½ **sweet red pepper, cut into thin strips**
1 **cup broccoli flowerets**
1 **(6-ounce) can sliced ripe olives**
1 **(8-ounce) bottle Italian salad dressing**

Cook rotini according to package directions; drain. Rinse pasta with cold water and drain.

Combine pasta and remaining ingredients, tossing well. Serve immediately or, if desired, chill. **Yield: 6 to 8 servings.**

Boiled Shrimp with Zippy Red Sauce

1 **cup chili sauce**
1 **cup ketchup**
2 **tablespoons prepared horseradish**
2 **tablespoons picante sauce**
3 **tablespoons lemon juice**
2 **tablespoons Worcestershire sauce**
1 **teaspoon onion powder**
1 **teaspoon garlic powder**
3 **pounds unpeeled, large boiled shrimp**

Combine first 8 ingredients, stirring well. Cover and chill at least 2 hours. Serve with boiled shrimp. **Yield: 6 servings.**

Onion-Cheese French Bread

¼ **cup butter or margarine, softened**
¾ **cup (3 ounces) shredded Cheddar cheese**
½ **cup mayonnaise**
¼ **cup chopped green onions**
1 **(16-ounce) loaf French bread**

Combine first 4 ingredients in a small bowl; mix well.

Slice bread in half lengthwise. Spread cheese mixture on bread. Broil 6 inches from heat (with electric oven door partially opened) 2 minutes or until bubbly. **Yield: 8 servings.**

All-in-One-Dish

Consider an easy approach to meal planning on hectic days. Our collection of all-in-one-dish combinations may be just what you need to simplify meal preparation and cleanup.

Szechuan Noodle Toss, Chicken and Vegetables, Shrimp Dee-Lish

Kielbasa-Vegetable Dinner, Linguine with Clam Sauce, Fish-and-Potato Platter

Lime-Ginger Beef Stir-Fry, Stir-Fry Beef and Asparagus, Sausage Ratatouille

Pork Marsala, Shrimp and Tortellini, Easy Red Beans and Rice

Turkey Sauté (page 36)

Quick Oriental Fix

SERVES 6
Szechuan Noodle Toss • Salad Mandarin
Breadsticks • Caramel Surprise

Szechuan Noodle Toss

Szechuan Noodle Toss

1 (8-ounce) package thin spaghetti
2 large sweet red peppers, cut into very thin
   strips
4 green onions, cut into 1-inch pieces
1 clove garlic, crushed
¼ cup sesame oil, divided
1 (10-ounce) package fresh, trimmed spinach,
   torn into bite-size pieces
2 cups cubed cooked chicken
1 (8-ounce) can sliced water chestnuts, drained
¼ cup soy sauce
2 tablespoons rice vinegar
1½ teaspoons dried crushed red pepper
1 tablespoon minced fresh gingerroot

Cook spaghetti according to package directions; drain. Rinse with cold water; drain. Place spaghetti in a large bowl; set aside.

Cook red pepper, green onions, and garlic in 2 tablespoons hot sesame oil in a large skillet, stirring constantly, 2 minutes. Stir in spinach; cover and cook over medium heat 3 minutes or until spinach wilts. Remove from heat; cool.

Spoon spinach mixture over pasta. Add chicken and water chestnuts.

Combine remaining 2 tablespoons sesame oil, soy sauce, and remaining ingredients; stir well. Pour over pasta, tossing gently to coat. **Yield: 6 servings.**

Salad Mandarin

1 medium head Bibb or Boston lettuce, torn
1 (11-ounce) can mandarin oranges, chilled
   and drained
½ medium avocado, peeled and thinly sliced
½ cup coarsely chopped pecans, toasted
2 green onions, thinly sliced
Freshly ground pepper to taste
⅓ cup commercial Italian dressing

Combine first 6 ingredients in a medium bowl. Add Italian dressing, tossing gently. **Yield: 6 servings.**

Caramel Surprise

1 quart vanilla ice cream
4 (1½-ounce) English toffee-flavored candy
   bars, frozen and crushed
¼ cup plus 2 tablespoons Kahlúa or other
   coffee-flavored liqueur

Spoon alternate layers of ice cream and crushed candy into 6 parfait glasses. Top each with 1 tablespoon Kahlúa. **Yield: 6 servings.**

TimeSavers

- Use leftover cooked chicken or buy cooked chicken from the deli for the noodle toss.
- Purchase pre-washed spinach, if available.
- Assemble dessert ahead of time and freeze; top with Kahlúa at serving time.

Skillet Dinner

SERVES 2

Chicken and Vegetables • Cheesy Pita Triangles
Individual Pots de Crème

Chicken and Vegetables

Chicken and Vegetables

2 carrots, scraped and sliced
¼ cup chopped onion
1 to 2 tablespoons vegetable oil
2 skinned and boned chicken breast halves,
     cut into ¼-inch strips
¼ teaspoon dried basil
¼ teaspoon garlic powder
⅛ teaspoon salt
⅛ teaspoon pepper
¼ cup chicken broth
2 tablespoons white wine
1 (6-ounce) package frozen snow pea pods,
     thawed and drained
1 medium tomato, cut into 8 pieces
⅓ cup minced fresh parsley

Cook carrot and onion in 1 tablespoon hot oil
in a large skillet over medium heat, stirring constantly, until crisp-tender. Remove vegetables
from skillet, reserving pan drippings.

Add chicken to skillet; sprinkle with basil,
garlic powder, salt, and pepper. Cook chicken 3
minutes on each side or until browned, adding 1
tablespoon oil if needed. Add reserved vegetables, chicken broth, and wine.

Cover, reduce heat, and simmer 10 minutes.
Stir in snow peas, tomato, and parsley; cook until
thoroughly heated. **Yield: 2 servings.**

TimeSavers

• Save time and nutrients by leaving peel on tomato. Substitute
cherry tomatoes, if desired.
• Press thawed snow peas between
paper towels to speed draining.
• Use kitchen shears to cut pita
bread into triangles.

Cheesy Pita Triangles

1 (8-inch) white or whole wheat pita bread
     round
¼ cup (1 ounce) shredded Swiss cheese

Cut pita bread round into 6 triangles; sprinkle
Swiss cheese inside each triangle, and place on a
baking sheet.

Bake at 350° for 10 minutes. Serve immediately. **Yield: 2 servings.**

Individual
Pots de Crème

½ (4-ounce) package sweet baking chocolate
2 tablespoons egg substitute
2 teaspoons sugar
¼ cup whipping cream
¼ teaspoon vanilla extract
Garnish: whipped cream

Melt chocolate in a heavy saucepan over low
heat. Combine egg substitute, sugar, and whipping cream; gradually stir into melted chocolate.

Cook over low heat, stirring constantly, 5
minutes or until thickened. Remove from heat;
stir in vanilla.

Spoon mixture into individual serving containers. Cover and chill at least 3 hours. Garnish, if
desired. **Yield: 2 servings.**

Spotlight Turkey Tonight
(pictured on page 31)
SERVES 4
Turkey Sauté • Buttered rice • ◆ Tomato-Herb Salad • Chocolate-Mint Dessert

Turkey Sauté

2   teaspoons cornstarch
2   tablespoons soy sauce
¼   cup water
1   teaspoon sugar
1   clove garlic, minced
½   teaspoon grated fresh gingerroot
2   tablespoons vegetable oil
1   pound turkey breast cutlets, cut into
      bite-size pieces
1   (6-ounce) package frozen snow pea pods,
      thawed
1   (8-ounce) can sliced water chestnuts,
      drained
½   small sweet red pepper, sliced

Combine first 4 ingredients; set aside. Cook garlic and gingerroot in hot oil in a large heavy skillet until tender.

Add turkey, and cook, stirring constantly, 3 minutes or until lightly browned. Add snow peas, water chestnuts, and red pepper slices; cook 1 minute, stirring constantly. Add soy sauce mixture, and cook 2 minutes or until thickened.
Yield: 4 servings.

TimeSavers

• Press thawed snow peas between paper towels to remove excess water.
• Allow tomatoes time to marinate for best flavor.
• Use bakery or deli brownies as the base for dessert.

Tomato-Herb Salad

3   small tomatoes, sliced
2   tablespoons vegetable oil
2   tablespoons white wine vinegar
½   teaspoon salt
¼   teaspoon pepper
2   tablespoons chopped fresh chives
Lettuce leaves

Arrange tomato in a 13- x 9- x 2-inch dish.
Combine oil and next 3 ingredients in a jar; cover tightly, and shake vigorously. Pour dressing over tomato. Sprinkle with chives. Cover and chill at least 2 hours. Serve on lettuce leaves.
Yield: 4 servings.

Chocolate-Mint Dessert

1   (5.5-ounce) can chocolate syrup
2   tablespoons green crème de menthe
Brownies
Vanilla or chocolate-mint ice cream

Combine chocolate syrup and crème de menthe, stirring well. Serve warm or cold over brownies topped with ice cream. **Yield: about** ⅔ cup sauce.

Lime-Ginger Beef Stir-Fry

1 (1-pound) top loin steak
¼ teaspoon freshly ground pepper
½ teaspoon grated lime rind
¼ cup lime juice
1 tablespoon sugar
2 tablespoons dry sherry
2 teaspoons soy sauce
1 teaspoon grated fresh gingerroot
1 clove garlic, minced
1 tablespoon safflower or vegetable oil
2 green onions, cut into 2-inch lengths
1 large carrot, cut into 1½-inch strips
1 sweet red pepper, cut into 1½-inch strips
1 tablespoon cornstarch
¼ cup water
Hot cooked rice
Garnish: lime slices

Slice steak diagonally across grain into thin strips; sprinkle with pepper, and set aside.

Combine lime rind and next 6 ingredients; set lime mixture aside.

Pour oil around top of preheated wok, coating sides; heat at medium-high (375°) for 1 minute. Add steak; stir-fry 2 to 3 minutes. Add vegetables; stir-fry 2 to 3 minutes. Add lime mixture, and stir-fry until mixture boils.

Combine cornstarch and water; stir into vegetables and bring to a boil, stirring constantly. Cook, stirring constantly, 1 minute. Serve over rice. Garnish, if desired. **Yield: 4 servings.**

Lime-Ginger Beef Stir-Fry

Cantaloupe Cooler Salad

3 cups cubed cantaloupe
Lettuce leaves
½ small onion, thinly sliced and separated
   into rings
6 slices bacon, cooked and crumbled
Commercial poppy seed dressing

Arrange cantaloupe on lettuce leaves. Top with onion and crumbled bacon. Drizzle dressing over salad. **Yield: 4 servings.**

Stir-Fry Beef and Asparagus

Dinner from a Wok

SERVES 4

Stir-Fry Beef and Asparagus • Quick Cheese and Mushroom Salad
Crusty rolls • ◆ Decadent Mud Pie

Stir-Fry Beef and Asparagus

1 pound boneless sirloin steak
1 tablespoon cornstarch, divided
3 tablespoons dry sherry, divided
3 tablespoons soy sauce, divided
1½ tablespoons vegetable oil
1 pound fresh asparagus, cut diagonally into
    1-inch lengths
3 tablespoons beef broth
Hot cooked rice

Slice steak diagonally across grain into thin strips; place in a shallow dish.

Combine 2 teaspoons cornstarch, 2 tablespoons sherry, and 2 tablespoons soy sauce; pour over steak, and marinate 10 minutes. Remove steak from marinade.

Pour oil around top of preheated wok, coating sides; heat at medium high (375°) for 2 minutes. Add steak; stir-fry 4 minutes. Remove steak from wok. Add asparagus and beef broth. Bring to a boil; cover, reduce heat, and simmer 3 minutes.

Combine remaining 1 teaspoon cornstarch, 1 tablespoon sherry, and 1 tablespoon soy sauce. Add cornstarch mixture and steak to wok; bring to a boil. Cook, stirring constantly, 1 minute. Serve over rice. **Yield: 4 servings.**

Quick Cheese and Mushroom Salad

2 cups torn Bibb lettuce
2 cups torn iceberg lettuce
6 slices bacon, cooked and crumbled
¼ pound sliced fresh mushrooms
⅓ cup grated Parmesan cheese
¾ cup (3 ounces) shredded Swiss cheese
Commercial creamy Italian salad dressing

Combine all ingredients, except dressing; toss gently. Serve with dressing. **Yield: 4 servings.**

Decadent Mud Pie

½ gallon coffee ice cream, softened
1 (9-inch) graham cracker crust
1 (11.75-ounce) jar hot fudge sauce, heated
Commercial whipped topping
Slivered almonds, toasted

Spread ice cream evenly over crust; cover and freeze until firm. To serve, place pie slice on serving plate; spoon hot fudge sauce over each slice. Dollop with whipped topping, and sprinkle with toasted almonds. Serve immediately. **Yield: one 9-inch pie.**

TimeSavers

• For easier slicing of the steak, freeze it 30 to 60 minutes. Slicing steak across the grain makes it more tender. Position the knife at a 45° angle for attractive slices.
• Choose asparagus stalks that are uniform in size to ensure even cooking. The tough part of an asparagus spear will snap off when you bend the spear.

Pork with a Flair
SERVES 4
Pork Marsala • Garlic-Tarragon Green Salad • French rolls
♦ Mellowed-Out Melon Compotes

Pork Marsala

1 (1-pound) pork tenderloin
1 tablespoon butter or margarine
1 tablespoon vegetable oil
1 clove garlic, minced
½ cup marsala
½ cup dry red wine
1 tablespoon tomato paste
½ pound fresh mushroom caps
1 tablespoon chopped fresh parsley
Hot cooked noodles or rice

Cut tenderloin into 4 equal pieces. Place each piece between two sheets of heavy-duty plastic wrap, and flatten to ¼-inch thickness, using a meat mallet or rolling pin.

Heat butter and oil in a large, heavy skillet over medium heat. Add pork, and cook 3 to 4 minutes on each side or until browned. Remove pork from skillet, and keep warm.

Cook garlic in pan drippings in skillet; add wines and tomato paste, stirring until blended. Add mushroom caps, and simmer 3 to 5 minutes.

Return pork to skillet, and cook until thoroughly heated. Sprinkle with parsley, and serve over noodles or rice. **Yield: 4 servings.**

Garlic-Tarragon Green Salad

1 clove garlic, minced
¼ teaspoon salt
⅛ teaspoon freshly ground pepper
Pinch of dry mustard
1 tablespoon tarragon vinegar
¼ cup vegetable oil
8 cups mixed salad greens

Combine first 4 ingredients in a large bowl; blend with a fork. Add vinegar and oil, mixing well. Add lettuce; toss gently. **Yield: 4 to 6 servings.**

Mellowed-Out Melon Compotes

1½ cups cubed cantaloupe
1½ cups cubed honeydew melon
¼ cup amaretto
½ cup slivered almonds, toasted

Combine first 3 ingredients; toss gently to coat. Chill 1 hour. Spoon into individual compotes; sprinkle with almonds, and serve immediately. **Yield: 4 servings.**

TimeSavers

- To clean mushrooms, brush with a damp paper towel or place in a plastic salad spinner for quick rinsing and drying.
- Mince garlic for the entrée and salad at the same time.
- Keep a tube of tomato paste in the refrigerator to use when you need a small amount.
- Buy cut-up melon in the produce section.

Pork Marsala

Kielbasa-Vegetable Dinner

Busy Day Dinner

SERVES 6

Kielbasa-Vegetable Dinner • ◆ Spoon Rolls • Tart Lemon Pie

Kielbasa-Vegetable Dinner

3 slices bacon
1½ pounds small red potatoes, thinly sliced
1 cup chopped onion
1½ cups thinly sliced carrot
½ teaspoon dried marjoram
1½ pounds kielbasa sausage, cut into ½-inch slices
1½ pounds fresh broccoli flowerets
1 cup water

Cook bacon in a large Dutch oven until crisp; remove bacon, reserving drippings in Dutch oven. Crumble bacon, and set aside.

Cook potato, onion, carrot, and marjoram in reserved drippings in Dutch oven over medium heat 7 minutes, stirring often.

Add kielbasa, broccoli, and water to vegetables in Dutch oven; bring mixture to a boil. Cover, reduce heat, and simmer 15 minutes or until vegetables are crisp-tender, stirring occasionally. Spoon into soup bowls; sprinkle with bacon. **Yield: 6 servings.**

TimeSavers

• To save time, use frozen chopped onion, and buy broccoli flowerets and scraped baby carrots from the produce section.
• Wash the potatoes well, but leave the skins on to save time and preserve nutrients.
• Make batter for rolls ahead of time.

Spoon Rolls

1 package active dry yeast
2 tablespoons warm water (105° to 115°)
½ cup vegetable oil
¼ cup sugar
1 large egg, beaten
4 cups self-rising flour
2 cups warm water (105° to 115°)

Dissolve yeast in 2 tablespoons warm water in a large bowl; let stand 5 minutes. Add oil and remaining ingredients to yeast mixture, and stir until mixture is smooth.

Cover; chill at least 4 hours or up to 3 days.

Stir batter, and spoon into greased muffin pans, filling three-fourths full. Bake at 400° for 20 minutes or until golden. **Yield: 1½ dozen.**

Tart Lemon Pie

3 large eggs
1 medium lemon, unpeeled, quartered, and seeded
1¼ cups sugar
2 tablespoons lemon juice
¼ cup butter or margarine, melted
1 unbaked 9-inch pastry shell
Frozen whipped topping, thawed

Combine first 4 ingredients in an electric blender; process 3 minutes or until smooth. Add butter; process 30 seconds. Pour into pastry shell. Bake at 350° for 30 to 35 minutes. Serve pie at room temperature or chilled with whipped topping. **Yield: one 9-inch pie.**

Sausage Ratatouille

One-Dish Dinner for Two

SERVES 2

Sausage Ratatouille • ◆ Mixed Greens with Blue Cheese Vinaigrette
Breadsticks • ◆ Grasshopper Tarts

Sausage Ratatouille

½ pound Italian sausage
1 small onion, chopped
¼ cup olive oil
1 small eggplant (¾ pound), cut into ½-inch
   cubes
1 zucchini, sliced
1 clove garlic, minced
1 large tomato, peeled and chopped
½ teaspoon dried oregano
¼ teaspoon salt
¼ teaspoon pepper
Garnish: fresh parsley sprigs

Remove casings from sausage. Cook sausage
in a large skillet over medium heat until browned,
stirring to crumble. Drain well; set aside.

Cook onion in hot oil in a large skillet over
medium heat, stirring constantly, until tender.
Add eggplant, and cook 3 minutes, stirring constantly. Add zucchini and garlic; reduce heat, and
simmer 10 minutes. Add tomato, sausage, and
seasonings; cover and simmer 5 minutes, stirring
once. Garnish, if desired. **Yield: 2 servings.**

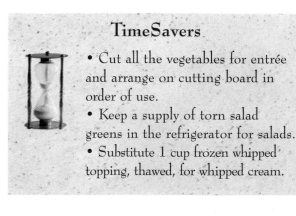

TimeSavers

• Cut all the vegetables for entrée
and arrange on cutting board in
order of use.
• Keep a supply of torn salad
greens in the refrigerator for salads.
• Substitute 1 cup frozen whipped
topping, thawed, for whipped cream.

Mixed Greens with Blue Cheese Vinaigrette

¼ cup vegetable oil
1½ tablespoons white wine vinegar
1 ounce crumbled blue cheese
½ teaspoon dried oregano
⅛ teaspoon salt
⅛ teaspoon freshly ground pepper
1 cup torn radicchio
1 cup torn Bibb lettuce

Combine first 6 ingredients in a jar; cover
tightly and shake. Chill at least 1 hour.

Place salad greens in a bowl. Toss with dressing just before serving. **Yield: 2 servings.**

Grasshopper Tarts

⅔ cup chocolate wafer crumbs
1 tablespoon butter or margarine, melted
½ cup marshmallow cream
1 tablespoon green crème de menthe
½ cup whipping cream, whipped

Combine chocolate wafer crumbs and butter;
press onto the bottom and sides of 2 (6-ounce)
freezerproof ramekins. Chill 1 hour.

Combine marshmallow cream and crème de
menthe, stirring well. Set aside 2 tablespoons
whipped cream; fold remaining whipped cream
into marshmallow mixture.

Spoon into prepared crusts; top with reserved
whipped cream. Cover loosely, and freeze at least
8 hours. **Yield: 2 servings.**

Fireside Supper

SERVES 4 TO 6
Easy Red Beans and Rice • ◆ Overnight Slaw
Quick Corn Muffins • Citrus fruit cup

Easy Red Beans and Rice

1 pound smoked link sausage, cut into ½-inch
    slices
1 medium onion, chopped
1 green pepper, chopped
1 clove garlic, minced
2 (15-ounce) cans kidney beans, drained
1 (16-ounce) can whole tomatoes, undrained
    and chopped
½ teaspoon dried oregano
½ teaspoon pepper
Hot cooked rice

    Cook sausage over low heat 5 to 8 minutes.
Add onion, green pepper, and garlic; cook until
tender. Drain, if necessary. Add beans, tomatoes,
and seasonings; simmer, uncovered, 20 minutes.
Serve over rice. **Yield: 4 to 6 servings.**

Overnight Slaw

5 cups shredded cabbage
¼ cup chopped purple onion
¾ cup sugar
¾ cup white vinegar
¾ cup water
2 teaspoons salt

    Combine cabbage and purple onion in a large
bowl. Combine sugar and remaining ingredients,
stirring until sugar dissolves. Pour over cabbage
mixture; toss gently.
    Cover and chill 8 hours. Serve with a slotted
spoon. **Yield: 4 to 6 servings.**

Quick Corn Muffins

1 (8½-ounce) package corn muffin mix
2 tablespoons chopped onion
1 large egg, beaten
⅓ cup milk

    Combine muffin mix and onion; add egg and
milk, stirring just until dry ingredients are moistened. Pour batter into well-greased muffin pans,
filling two-thirds full. Bake at 400° for 15 minutes or until lightly browned. **Yield: 6 to 8
muffins.**

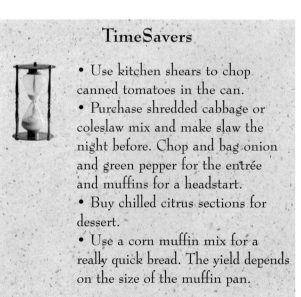

TimeSavers

• Use kitchen shears to chop
canned tomatoes in the can.
• Purchase shredded cabbage or
coleslaw mix and make slaw the
night before. Chop and bag onion
and green pepper for the entrée
and muffins for a headstart.
• Buy chilled citrus sections for
dessert.
• Use a corn muffin mix for a
really quick bread. The yield depends
on the size of the muffin pan.

Easy Red Beans and Rice

Simple and Sensational

SERVES 4

Shrimp and Tortellini • Asparagus with Garlic Butter
Crusty Italian bread • Orange-Glazed Bananas Foster

Shrimp and Tortellini

Shrimp and Tortellini

1 (9-ounce) package refrigerated
    cheese-filled tortellini, uncooked
⅓ cup butter or margarine
1 pound peeled, medium-size fresh shrimp
1 shallot, minced
2 tablespoons chopped fresh basil or
    2 teaspoons dried basil
½ cup grated Parmesan cheese
Garnish: fresh basil

Cook pasta according to package directions; drain and set aside.

Melt butter in a large skillet over medium-high heat; add shrimp, minced shallot, and chopped basil. Cook, stirring constantly, about 5 minutes. Add pasta and Parmesan cheese. Toss gently, and garnish, if desired. **Yield: 4 servings.**

Orange-Glazed Bananas Foster

2 bananas, split and quartered
⅓ cup orange juice
2 tablespoons Grand Marnier or other
    orange-flavored liqueur
1 tablespoon butter or margarine
2 tablespoons chopped walnuts
2 tablespoons firmly packed brown sugar
Vanilla ice cream

Arrange bananas in an 8-inch square baking dish. Combine orange juice and liqueur; pour over bananas, and dot with butter. Bake at 400° for 10 minutes, basting occasionally.

Combine walnuts and brown sugar; sprinkle over bananas, and bake 5 additional minutes. Serve immediately over ice cream. **Yield: 4 servings.**

Asparagus with Garlic Butter

1 pound fresh asparagus or 1 (10-ounce)
    package frozen asparagus
1½ tablespoons butter
1 clove garlic, minced
½ teaspoon soy sauce

Cut asparagus on the diagonal into 2-inch pieces.
Cook asparagus, covered, in a small amount of boiling water 4 minutes or until crisp-tender; drain.

Melt butter in a large saucepan, and add garlic and soy sauce. Cook over low heat, stirring constantly, 1 minute. Add asparagus; toss to coat. **Yield: 4 servings.**

TimeSavers

• Buy a wedge of fresh Parmesan cheese, and ask the deli personnel to grate it for you.
• Substitute 2 green onions for 1 shallot, if desired.
• Add a drop of vegetable oil to the pasta water to prevent it from boiling over.
• Choose asparagus stalks that are uniform in size to ensure even cooking.

Fast Shrimp Dee-Lish

SERVES 4

Shrimp Dee-Lish • Tomato-Asparagus Salad
Chive-Garlic French Bread • Lemon sherbet

Shrimp Dee-Lish

Vegetable cooking spray
1 cup sliced green onions
½ cup chopped celery
½ cup sliced fresh mushrooms
4 cloves garlic, minced
1 pound peeled, medium-size fresh shrimp
1 (10¾-ounce) can cream of mushroom soup, undiluted
¼ teaspoon Creole seasoning
1 (8-ounce) carton plain yogurt
Hot cooked noodles
Garnish: green onion fan

Coat a large nonstick skillet with cooking spray; place over medium heat until hot. Add green onions and next 3 ingredients; cook until vegetables are tender.

Add shrimp; cook 5 minutes, stirring constantly. Stir in soup and seasoning; bring to a boil.

Remove from heat; stir in yogurt (at room temperature), and serve immediately over noodles. Garnish, if desired. **Yield: 4 servings.**

Tomato-Asparagus Salad

1 pound fresh asparagus
8 romaine lettuce leaves
12 cherry tomatoes, halved
⅓ cup commercial Italian salad dressing
¼ cup grated Parmesan cheese

Snap off tough ends of asparagus. Place asparagus in steaming rack over boiling water;

cover and steam 4 minutes. Drain and plunge into ice water to cool. Drain asparagus well.

Arrange lettuce leaves on individual plates. Arrange asparagus spears and tomato on top; drizzle with salad dressing, and sprinkle with Parmesan cheese. **Yield: 4 servings.**

Note: 1 (16-ounce) can asparagus spears may be substituted for fresh asparagus.

Chive-Garlic French Bread

¼ cup butter or margarine, softened
1 tablespoon minced chives
1 large clove garlic, minced
1 teaspoon lemon juice
10 (1-inch) slices French bread

Combine first 4 ingredients; spread on one side of bread slices. Place buttered side up on a baking sheet. Broil 6 inches from heat (with electric oven door partially opened) 2 to 3 minutes or until lightly browned. **Yield: 10 servings.**

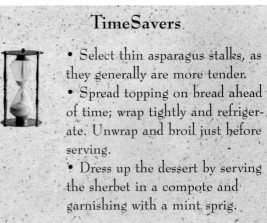

TimeSavers

• Select thin asparagus stalks, as they generally are more tender.
• Spread topping on bread ahead of time; wrap tightly and refrigerate. Unwrap and broil just before serving.
• Dress up the dessert by serving the sherbet in a compote and garnishing with a mint sprig.

Shrimp Dee-Lish

Linguine with Clam Sauce

Late Night Supper

SERVES 4 TO 6

Linguine with Clam Sauce • Spinach-Pecan Salad • Crusty Italian bread
◆ Crème de Menthe Parfait

Linguine with Clam Sauce

1 (16-ounce) package linguine
2 cloves garlic, minced
½ cup butter or margarine, melted
2 (6½-ounce) cans minced clams, drained
½ teaspoon dried basil
½ teaspoon dried oregano
¼ teaspoon salt
¼ teaspoon pepper
½ cup chopped fresh parsley
1 cup grated Parmesan cheese

Cook linguine in a Dutch oven according to package directions. Drain and return to Dutch oven; set aside.

Cook garlic in butter in a medium skillet; add clams and next 4 ingredients. Cook over low heat, stirring constantly, 5 minutes. Pour over hot cooked linguine; add parsley, and toss gently. Place on a warm platter, and top with Parmesan cheese. **Yield: 4 to 6 servings.**

Spinach-Pecan Salad

1 cup sliced mushrooms
½ cup commercial Italian salad dressing
1 (10-ounce) package fresh, trimmed spinach, torn into bite-size pieces
⅓ cup golden raisins
⅓ cup coarsely chopped pecans
2 hard-cooked eggs

Toss mushrooms with salad dressing; set aside.

Combine spinach, mushrooms, raisins, and pecans in a bowl; toss gently. Add additional dressing, if necessary. Grate egg over salad before serving. **Yield: 6 servings.**

Crème de Menthe Parfait

1 quart vanilla ice cream, softened
1 pint lime sherbet, softened
½ (8-ounce) carton frozen whipped topping, thawed
¼ cup green crème de menthe

Combine all ingredients in container of an electric blender; blend at medium speed until well mixed.

Spoon into parfait glasses. Place parfaits in freezer 3 to 4 hours. **Yield: 6 servings.**

TimeSavers

• To make cleanup easier when grating Parmesan cheese, brush grater lightly with oil before you start.
• Cook linguine in a Dutch oven with plenty of water so pasta has room to move around while cooking.
• Speed up salad preparation by buying pre-washed spinach, sliced mushrooms, and chopped pecans.

Dinner on a Platter

SERVES 4

Fish-and-Potato Platter • Fresh fruit with poppy seed dressing
◆ Peanut Butter Pie

Fish-and-Potato Platter

1 (8-ounce) carton plain nonfat yogurt
¼ cup chopped fresh dill
2 tablespoons rice vinegar
2 tablespoons chopped chives
½ teaspoon salt
½ teaspoon pepper
¾ pound small red potatoes, unpeeled and cut
    into ⅛-inch slices
1 pound salmon or amberjack fillets, skinned
    and cut crosswise into 3- x 1½-inch pieces
1 cup broccoli flowerets
2 tablespoons lemon juice

Combine first 6 ingredients in a small bowl;
cover and chill.

Overlap potato slices around edge of a
microwave-safe, round 12-inch platter. Cover
tightly with heavy-duty plastic wrap; fold back a
small edge of wrap to allow steam to escape.
Microwave at HIGH 3 minutes.

Uncover and place fish in a ring inside potato
slices with pieces end to end. Mound broccoli in
center of platter. Sprinkle fish and potato with
lemon juice; cover.

Microwave at HIGH 8 minutes or until fish is
cooked through and potato is tender, giving dish a
half-turn at 4-minute intervals. Serve with dill
sauce. **Yield: 4 servings.**

Fish-and-Potato Platter

Peanut Butter Pie

1 (8-ounce) package cream cheese, softened
1 cup sifted powdered sugar
1 cup chunky peanut butter
½ cup milk
1 (8-ounce) carton frozen whipped topping,
    thawed
1 (9-inch) graham cracker crust
¼ cup coarsely chopped peanuts

Combine first 4 ingredients in a bowl; beat at
medium speed of an electric mixer until blended.
Fold in whipped topping. Spoon into crust; sprinkle with peanuts. Chill. **Yield: one 9-inch pie.**

Make It Casual

Casual fare shouldn't take more time to make than to eat. These favorites stand on their own as hassle-free lunches or dinners.

Chili-Chicken Stew, Creamy Onion-and-Potato Soup, Stromboli

Caesar Salad with Tortellini and Asparagus, Crab Bisque, Feta-Tomato Crostini

Mexican Chef Salad, Ham-Pecan-Blue Cheese Pasta Salad, Double-Decker BLT

Honey-Mustard Turkey Salad, Ranch-Style Turkey 'n' Pasta Salad

Tuna-Pasta Salad (page 67)

Chili-Chicken Stew

Winter Warm-Up

SERVES 6

Chili-Chicken Stew • Deli coleslaw
Seasoned Cornbread • Brownie Chip Cookies

Chili-Chicken Stew

6 skinned, boned chicken breast halves
1 medium onion, chopped
1 medium-size green pepper, chopped
2 cloves garlic, minced
1 tablespoon vegetable oil
2 (14½-ounce) cans stewed tomatoes,
     undrained and chopped
1 (15-ounce) can pinto beans, drained
⅔ cup picante sauce
1 teaspoon chili powder
1 teaspoon ground cumin
½ teaspoon salt
Shredded Cheddar cheese, diced avocado,
     sliced green onions, and sour cream

Cut chicken into 1-inch pieces. Cook chicken, onion, green pepper, and garlic in hot oil in a Dutch oven until lightly browned. Add tomatoes and next 5 ingredients; cover, reduce heat, and simmer 20 minutes.

Top individual servings with remaining ingredients. **Yield: 6 servings.**

TimeSavers

• Use kitchen shears to chop tomatoes in the can and to cut chicken into uniform pieces.
• Buy chopped vegetables, shredded cheese, and deli coleslaw.
• Bake cookies in advance, or serve bakery cookies.

Seasoned Cornbread

1 (8½-ounce) package corn muffin mix
½ teaspoon poultry seasoning
1 large egg, beaten
⅔ cup milk

Combine muffin mix and poultry seasoning; add egg and milk, stirring just until dry ingredients are moistened. Pour batter into a well-greased 8-inch square baking dish; bake at 400° for 18 to 20 minutes. **Yield: 9 servings.**

Brownie Chip Cookies

1 (23.7-ounce) package brownie mix
2 large eggs
⅓ cup vegetable oil
1 (6-ounce) package semisweet chocolate
     morsels
½ cup chopped pecans

Combine brownie mix, eggs, and oil; beat about 50 strokes with a spoon. Stir in chocolate morsels and pecans. Drop dough by rounded teaspoonfuls onto greased cookie sheets.

Bake at 350° for 10 to 12 minutes. Cool slightly on cookie sheets; then remove to wire racks, and cool completely. **Yield: about 6 dozen.**

Soup & Salad, Anytime Meal

SERVES 6

Creamy Onion-and-Potato Soup • Spinach Salad
Ham-Cheese Biscuits • Red and green grapes

Creamy Onion-and-Potato Soup

2 tablespoons butter or margarine
2 tablespoons all-purpose flour
1 cup chopped onion
1 large clove garlic, minced
2 (14½-ounce) cans ready-to-serve chicken
   broth
4 cups peeled, cubed potato (about 3 large)
½ cup sliced green onions
⅛ teaspoon salt
¼ teaspoon ground white pepper
1 cup milk
Garnish: green onion strips

Melt butter in a Dutch oven over low heat; add flour, stirring until smooth. Cook, stirring constantly, 1 minute. Add onion and garlic; cook 1 minute or until onion is tender. Gradually add broth, stirring constantly. Add potato and next 3 ingredients.

Bring to a boil; cover, reduce heat, and simmer 15 minutes, stirring occasionally, or until potato is tender. Stir in milk, and heat thoroughly. Garnish, if desired. **Yield: 7 cups.**

TimeSavers

- Cut potatoes into small cubes to help them cook faster.
- Buy prewashed spinach, if available.
- Use leftover cooked ham for biscuits.

Spinach Salad

1 (10-ounce) package fresh, trimmed
   spinach
1 cup strawberries, halved
1 cup pecan halves, toasted
Commercial poppy seed dressing

Tear spinach leaves into bite-size pieces.
Combine spinach, strawberries, and pecans; drizzle with poppy seed dressing. Serve immediately. **Yield: 6 servings.**

Ham-Cheese Biscuits

2 cups biscuit mix
½ cup minced cooked ham
½ cup (2 ounces) shredded Cheddar cheese
⅔ cup milk

Combine first 3 ingredients in a medium bowl, stirring well. Sprinkle milk over dry mixture, stirring just until moistened.

Pat dough out onto a floured surface to ½-inch thickness; cut with a 2-inch biscuit cutter.

Place biscuits on a greased baking sheet. Bake at 450° for 8 minutes or until lightly browned. **Yield: 14 biscuits.**

Creamy Onion-and-Potato Soup

Mexican Chef Salad

A Taste of Tex-Mex

SERVES 4

Mexican Chef Salad • Strawberry Fool
Southern Sangría

Mexican Chef Salad

1 pound ground beef
¾ cup water
1 (1¼-ounce) package taco seasoning mix
8 cups torn iceberg lettuce
1 (16-ounce) can kidney beans, drained and
    rinsed
2 tomatoes, chopped
1 (2¼-ounce) can sliced ripe olives, drained
½ cup (2 ounces) shredded Cheddar cheese
Commercial guacamole
Tortilla chips

Cook ground beef in a skillet until meat is
browned, stirring to crumble; drain. Return meat
to skillet; add water and taco seasoning mix. Bring
to a boil; reduce heat, and simmer 10 minutes,
stirring occasionally.

Layer lettuce, beans, beef mixture, tomato,
olives, and cheese. Serve with guacamole and
tortilla chips. **Yield: 4 servings.**

TimeSavers

• Buy shredded cheese, sliced ripe
olives, and guacamole for a headstart on the salad.

• To save time with dessert, substitute frozen strawberries for fresh,
and 2 cups frozen whipped topping, thawed, for whipped cream;
omit sugar.

Strawberry Fool

2 cups fresh strawberries, hulled
¼ cup sugar
1 cup whipping cream, whipped
Garnish: 4 fresh strawberries

Place 2 cups strawberries and sugar in
container of a food processor or electric blender,
and process until smooth. Pour mixture into a
large bowl.

Fold whipped cream into strawberry mixture.
Spoon into individual serving bowls. Garnish, if
desired. Serve immediately, or chill 1 hour.
Yield: 4 servings.

Southern Sangría

⅓ cup sugar
⅓ cup lemon juice
⅓ cup orange juice
1 (25.4-ounce) bottle sparkling red grape
    juice, chilled

Combine first 3 ingredients in a large pitcher,
stirring until sugar dissolves. Add grape juice,
and gently stir to mix well. Serve over crushed
ice. **Yield: 5 cups.**

Ham-Pecan-Blue Cheese Pasta Salad

Lazy Day Fare

SERVES 6

Ham-Pecan-Blue Cheese Pasta Salad • ◆ Marinated Tomatoes
Crusty rolls • Blueberries and Cointreau

Ham-Pecan-Blue Cheese Pasta Salad

3 cups farfalle (bow tie pasta), uncooked
4 ounces cooked ham, cut into strips
1 cup coarsely chopped pecans
1 (4-ounce) package crumbled blue cheese
2 tablespoons chopped fresh parsley
1 tablespoon minced fresh rosemary or
    1 teaspoon dried rosemary
1 clove garlic, minced
½ teaspoon coarsely ground pepper
¼ cup olive oil
⅓ cup grated Parmesan cheese

Cook pasta according to package directions; drain. Rinse with cold water and drain.

Combine pasta and remaining ingredients except Parmesan cheese, tossing well. Sprinkle with Parmesan cheese. Serve immediately or chill, if desired. **Yield: 6 servings.**

TimeSavers

• Rinse cooked pasta in cold water to eliminate chilling salad if you plan to serve it immediately.
• Buy vine-ripened tomatoes and store at room temperature. To speed the ripening process, place tomatoes in a paper bag.
• To chop parsley, place in a glass measuring cup and snip with kitchen shears.

Marinated Tomatoes

3 large tomatoes
⅓ cup olive oil
¼ cup red wine vinegar
1 teaspoon salt
¼ teaspoon pepper
½ clove garlic, crushed
1 tablespoon chopped fresh parsley
1 tablespoon chopped fresh basil or
    1 teaspoon dried basil
2 tablespoons chopped onion

Cut tomatoes into ½-inch-thick slices, and arrange in a large shallow dish; set aside.

Combine remaining ingredients in a jar; cover tightly, and shake vigorously. Pour over tomato slices. Cover and marinate in refrigerator several hours. **Yield: 6 servings.**

Blueberries and Cointreau

3 cups fresh blueberries, rinsed and drained
¼ cup plus 2 tablespoons Cointreau or other
    orange-flavored liqueur
Sweetened whipped cream

Place ½ cup blueberries in each of 6 stemmed glasses; pour 1 tablespoon Cointreau over each serving.

Top each serving with a dollop of sweetened whipped cream. **Yield: 6 servings.**

Sunday Night Supper

Honey-Mustard Turkey Salad

2 cups chopped cooked turkey
6 slices bacon, cooked and crumbled
1 (4.5-ounce) jar whole mushrooms, drained
¼ cup sweet red pepper strips
¼ cup sliced green onions
½ cup mayonnaise or salad dressing
2 tablespoons honey
1½ tablespoons Dijon mustard
¾ teaspoon soy sauce
¾ teaspoon lemon juice
1 (2-ounce) package roasted cashews
Lettuce leaves
Sweet red pepper rings
Chow mein noodles

Combine first 5 ingredients in a medium bowl; set aside. Combine mayonnaise and next 4 ingredients; fold into turkey mixture. Cover and chill. Just before serving, stir in cashews. Serve on lettuce leaves and red pepper rings; sprinkle with chow mein noodles. **Yield: 4 servings.**

TimeSavers

• Use leftover cooked turkey or sliced turkey from the deli.
• Get a headstart on the salad by cooking extra breakfast bacon; wrap bacon airtight, and chill up to 5 days or freeze up to 6 weeks.
• Chop canned tomatoes right in the can with kitchen shears.

Creamy Tomato Soup

1 (10¾-ounce) can tomato soup, undiluted
1 (12-ounce) can evaporated milk
1 (14½-ounce) can stewed tomatoes, undrained and chopped
½ cup (2 ounces) shredded Cheddar cheese

Combine soup and milk in a medium saucepan, stirring with a wire whisk. Add tomatoes and cheese.

Cook over low heat until cheese melts and soup is hot. **Yield: 4⅔ cups.**

Sesame Knots

1 (11-ounce) package refrigerated soft breadsticks
2 tablespoons butter or margarine, melted
½ teaspoon sesame seeds or poppy seeds

Separate dough, and loosely tie each piece of dough into a knot. Arrange rolls 1 inch apart on an ungreased baking sheet. Brush with butter; sprinkle with sesame seeds.

Bake at 350° for 15 minutes or until golden brown. **Yield: 10 servings.**

Honey-Mustard Turkey Salad

Cool Summer Lunch
SERVES 6 TO 8
◆ Ranch-Style Turkey 'n' Pasta Salad • Crusty hard rolls • ◆ Green Grapes Surprise

Ranch-Style Turkey 'n' Pasta Salad

Ranch-Style Turkey 'n' Pasta Salad

2 cups penne pasta, uncooked
2 cups chopped cooked turkey
1 small zucchini, sliced
2 small yellow squash, sliced
1 small green pepper, chopped
1 small sweet red pepper, chopped
¼ cup grated Parmesan cheese
¾ cup commercial Ranch-style dressing

Cook pasta according to package directions; drain. Rinse with cold water; drain.

Combine pasta and remaining ingredients in a large bowl. Cover and chill at least 2 hours. Toss before serving. **Yield: 6 to 8 servings.**

Green Grapes Surprise

¼ cup firmly packed light brown sugar
½ cup sour cream
5 cups seedless green grapes, washed and stemmed
Garnish: mint sprigs

Combine brown sugar and sour cream in a large bowl. Stir in grapes. Chill several hours.

Spoon into individual serving dishes. Garnish, if desired. **Yield: 6 to 8 servings.**

An Autumn Favorite

(pictured on page 55)

SERVES 6

◆ Tuna-Pasta Salad • Fresh fruit with Tangy Coconut Dressing • Cheesy Twists

Tuna-Pasta Salad

6 ounces spinach or tri-colored corkscrew
      noodles, uncooked
½ cup sliced green onions
½ cup sweet yellow or green pepper strips
½ cup sliced ripe olives
1 cup halved cherry tomatoes
1 carrot, scraped and shredded
2 (6½-ounce) cans chunk light tuna, drained
      and flaked
½ cup vegetable oil
3 tablespoons white wine vinegar
2 tablespoons lemon juice
3 tablespoons minced fresh parsley
½ teaspoon salt
¼ teaspoon pepper
1 green onion, cut into 1-inch pieces
1 large clove garlic, halved
Lettuce leaves

   Cook pasta according to package directions;
drain. Rinse with cold water; drain. Combine
pasta and next 6 ingredients; set aside.
   Combine oil and remaining ingredients except
lettuce leaves in an electric blender, and process
until mixture is smooth.
   Pour dressing over salad, and toss gently.
Cover and chill at least 8 hours, stirring occasionally. Spoon salad over lettuce leaves, using a
slotted spoon. **Yield: 6 to 8 servings.**

Tangy Coconut Dressing

1 (15-ounce) can cream of coconut
1 (6-ounce) can frozen lemonade concentrate,
      thawed and undiluted

   Combine ingredients, stirring until blended.
Serve over fresh fruit. Store remaining dressing
in refrigerator. **Yield: about 2 cups.**

Cheesy Twists

½ cup grated Parmesan cheese
3 tablespoons butter or margarine, softened
½ teaspoon Dijon mustard
1 (10-ounce) can refrigerated buttermilk
      biscuits

   Combine first 3 ingredients; set aside.
   Roll each biscuit into a 5- x 2-inch rectangle;
spread about 2 teaspoons cheese mixture over
rectangle, and cut in half lengthwise. Twist each
strip 2 or 3 times, and place on a lightly greased
baking sheet.
   Bake at 400° for 8 to 10 minutes or until golden.
Yield: 20 twists.

TimeSavers

• Buy precut vegetables to shorten
salad preparation time.
• Remove frozen lemonade from
can, and thaw in the microwave.

Summertime Supper

SERVES 4

Caesar Salad with Tortellini and Asparagus • Mayonnaise Muffins
◆ Summer Fruit Compote

Caesar Salad with Tortellini and Asparagus

Caesar Salad with Tortellini and Asparagus

4 cups hot water
1 (9-ounce) package refrigerated cheese-filled tortellini, uncooked
½ pound fresh asparagus, cut into 2-inch pieces
¼ cup lemon juice
3 tablespoons olive oil
2 tablespoons water
1 tablespoon Worcestershire sauce
¼ teaspoon freshly ground pepper
1 clove garlic, pressed
1 head romaine lettuce, torn
¼ cup grated Parmesan cheese

Bring water to a boil in a 4-quart Dutch oven.

Add tortellini and asparagus, and cook 4 minutes. Drain; rinse in cold water and drain. Set mixture aside.

Combine lemon juice and next 5 ingredients, stirring with a wire whisk; set aside.

Place lettuce, tortellini, and asparagus in a large bowl; add dressing, tossing gently. Sprinkle with cheese. **Yield: 4 servings.**

TimeSavers

• To boil pasta faster, start with hot water. Cook pasta and asparagus together in the same pot.
• Buy sliced fruit in the produce section for fruit compote.
• Grate the lime for compote before squeezing it. Get more juice by microwaving the lime at HIGH 20 seconds before squeezing.

Mayonnaise Muffins

1 cup self-rising flour
2 tablespoons mayonnaise
½ cup milk

Combine all ingredients; stir until smooth.

Spoon batter into greased muffin pans, filling two-thirds full. Bake at 425° for 10 to 12 minutes. **Yield: 6 muffins.**

Summer Fruit Compote

¼ cup sugar
2 tablespoons rum
1 teaspoon grated lime rind
2 tablespoons fresh lime juice
1 nectarine
1 plum
1 pear
1 peach
4 strawberries

Combine first 4 ingredients. Seed and slice nectarine, plum, and pear; peel, seed, and slice peach. Pour dressing over fruit in a medium bowl; toss lightly. Cover and chill thoroughly.

Spoon into individual compotes; top each serving with a strawberry. **Yield: 4 servings.**

Patio Supper

SERVES 4

Stromboli • ♦ Marinated Artichoke Salad
Potato chips • Dill pickles • Grape Juice-Fruit Refresher

Stromboli

1 (16-ounce) loaf frozen bread dough, thawed
¼ pound thinly sliced ham
¼ pound sliced hard salami
½ teaspoon dried basil, divided
½ teaspoon dried oregano, divided
3 ounces sliced provolone cheese
1 cup (4 ounces) shredded mozzarella cheese
2 tablespoons butter or margarine, melted
1 teaspoon cornmeal

Place bread dough on a lightly greased baking sheet; pat to a 15- x 10-inch rectangle. Arrange ham slices lengthwise down center; place salami on top. Sprinkle with ¼ teaspoon basil and ¼ teaspoon oregano. Arrange provolone cheese over herbs, and top with mozzarella cheese; sprinkle with remaining herbs.

Moisten all edges of dough with water. Bring each long edge of dough to center; press edges together securely to seal. Seal ends.

Brush dough with 1 tablespoon butter. Sprinkle with cornmeal, and carefully invert. Brush top with remaining butter. Bake at 375° for 20 to 22 minutes. **Yield: 4 servings.**

Marinated Artichoke Salad

1 (6-ounce) jar marinated artichoke hearts, undrained
1 (4-ounce) can sliced mushrooms, drained
1 (4-ounce) can sliced ripe olives, drained
½ cup chopped onion
2 stalks celery, sliced
1 medium tomato, cut into wedges
Lettuce leaves

Combine first 6 ingredients in a large bowl, stirring well. Cover and chill thoroughly.

Transfer salad with a slotted spoon into a lettuce-lined bowl. **Yield: 4 servings.**

Grape Juice-Fruit Refresher

1 quart pineapple or lime sherbet
1⅓ cups sliced fresh strawberries
¼ to ½ cup white grape juice

Spoon sherbet equally into 4 compotes. Top each with ⅓ cup sliced strawberries. Just before serving, pour 1 to 2 tablespoons grape juice over top. **Yield: 4 servings.**

TimeSavers

- Buy sliced meat and cheese at deli.
- Thaw frozen bread dough at room temperature, or follow quick thawing instructions on package.

Stromboli

Mexican Egg Salad Tacos

Quick-Fix Lunch

SERVES 6

Mexican Egg Salad Tacos • ◆ Herbed Tomatoes • Peach Crinkle

Mexican Egg Salad Tacos

4 large hard-cooked eggs, chopped
¼ cup (1 ounce) shredded sharp Cheddar cheese
1 tablespoon chopped green onions
2 tablespoons mayonnaise or salad dressing
2 tablespoons salsa
1 tablespoon sour cream
⅛ teaspoon salt
⅛ teaspoon pepper
6 taco shells
Lettuce leaves
¾ cup (3 ounces) shredded sharp Cheddar cheese
Avocado slices
Additional salsa

Combine first 3 ingredients in a medium bowl; set aside.

Combine mayonnaise and next 4 ingredients; fold into egg mixture.

Line taco shells with lettuce. Spoon egg salad evenly into taco shells. Sprinkle 2 tablespoons cheese on each taco. Serve with avocado slices and salsa. **Yield: 6 servings.**

Herbed Tomatoes

⅓ cup vegetable oil
2 tablespoons white wine vinegar
¼ cup chopped fresh parsley
¼ cup chopped fresh chives
⅛ teaspoon pepper
Pinch of dried thyme
3 tomatoes, unpeeled and quartered
Lettuce

Combine first 6 ingredients in a 2-cup glass measure; mix well. Place tomato in a shallow container; pour dressing over tomato. Cover and chill 8 hours or overnight.

Drain tomato, reserving dressing. Arrange tomato on lettuce leaves; spoon dressing over tomato. **Yield: 6 servings.**

Peach Crinkle

1 (29-ounce) can sliced peaches, drained
1 teaspoon grated lemon rind
1 (11-ounce) package piecrust mix
1 cup firmly packed brown sugar
¼ cup cold butter or margarine, cut into small pieces

Place peaches in a lightly greased 11- x 7- x 1½-inch baking dish. Sprinkle with lemon rind, and set aside.

Combine piecrust mix and sugar; sprinkle over top. Dot with butter.

Bake at 375° for 30 minutes. Serve with vanilla ice cream or frozen yogurt. **Yield: 6 servings.**

TimeSavers

• Save time and nutrients by not peeling tomatoes.
• To seed avocado, cut lengthwise all the way around and twist halves in opposite directions to separate. Remove seed; brush cut surface with lemon juice to keep from turning brown.

Relax with Soup and Sandwiches

SERVES 4
Double-Decker BLT • Pickles • Broccoli-Cheese Soup
Cookies and fresh fruit • Easy Mint Tea

Double-Decker BLT

1 (13-ounce) loaf unsliced French bread
Olive oil-flavored cooking spray
Garlic-Basil Mayonnaise
Salad greens
4 tomatoes, thinly sliced
16 slices bacon, cooked

Cut bread into 12 slices. Coat one side of each with cooking spray. Grill or toast until golden.

Spread Garlic-Basil Mayonnaise on other side of each bread slice; layer 4 slices with half each of salad greens, tomato slices, and bacon. Top each with a second bread slice and remaining salad greens, tomato, and bacon. Top with remaining bread slices. **Yield: 4 sandwiches.**

Garlic-Basil Mayonnaise
½ cup mayonnaise or salad dressing
1 tablespoon chopped fresh basil or
      1 teaspoon dried basil
¼ teaspoon garlic salt
¼ teaspoon freshly ground pepper

Combine all ingredients; cover and chill.
Yield: ½ cup.

TimeSavers

• Microwave bacon in advance on a microwave-safe rack or paper plate with a double layer of paper towels between each layer of slices. Cook 8 slices at HIGH 6 to 7 minutes.

Broccoli-Cheese Soup

¾ cup water
1 (10-ounce) package frozen chopped broccoli
1 (10¾-ounce) can cream of chicken soup
½ cup milk
⅛ teaspoon ground red pepper
½ cup (2 ounces) shredded Cheddar cheese

Bring water to a boil in a large saucepan; add broccoli. Cover, reduce heat, and simmer 5 minutes or until tender. Stir in soup and milk.

Cook over medium heat, stirring constantly, until thoroughly heated. Stir in pepper. Pour into serving bowls. Top each serving with cheese.
Yield: 1 quart.

Easy Mint Tea

2 cups boiling water
5 regular-size, mint-flavored tea bags
1 cup sugar
¾ cup lemon juice
1½ quarts water
1 cup pineapple juice
2 cups ginger ale

Pour boiling water over tea bags; cover and steep 5 minutes. Remove tea bags, squeezing gently. Add sugar and lemon juice, stirring until sugar dissolves. Stir in 1½ quarts water, pineapple juice, and ginger ale. Serve over ice. **Yield: about 3 quarts.**

Double-Decker BLT

Quick Gourmet Fare

SERVES 6

Feta-Tomato Crostini • Pita chips • Crab Bisque • Fresh fruit

Feta-Tomato Crostini

3 (6-inch) French bread rolls, split
Olive oil
1 (7-ounce) package feta cheese, crumbled
Coarse ground garlic powder with parsley
3 small tomatoes, chopped
1½ tablespoons balsamic vinegar
2 tablespoons chopped fresh mint
Lettuce leaves
Garnish: fresh mint sprigs

Brush cut side of each roll with olive oil; place on a baking sheet. Broil 6 inches from heat (with electric oven door partially opened) 2 minutes or until lightly browned.

Place crumbled cheese evenly on each roll; sprinkle lightly with garlic powder. Place tomato over cheese; drizzle with balsamic vinegar, and sprinkle with mint. Serve on lettuce leaves, and garnish, if desired. Serve immediately. **Yield: 6 servings.**

Feta-Tomato Crostini

TimeSavers

• Substitute red wine vinegar for balsamic vinegar in crostini, if desired.
• While bisque is heating, prepare crostini.

Crab Bisque

1 (10¾-ounce) can cream of mushroom soup, undiluted
1 (10¾-ounce) can cream of asparagus soup, undiluted
2 cups milk
1 cup half-and-half
1 (6-ounce) can crabmeat, drained and flaked
¼ to ⅓ cup Chablis or other dry white wine

Combine first 4 ingredients in a saucepan; cook over medium heat until thoroughly heated, stirring occasionally. Add crabmeat and wine; cook until thoroughly heated. **Yield: 6 cups.**

Kids' Favorites

When time is short and you need fresh ideas for picky eaters, try these no-fuss kid pleasers. They're just right for hectic times.

Strawberry-French Toast Sandwiches, Gulf Coast Fried Shrimp

Big Veggie Sandwich, Corn Chowder, Bacon-Cheese French Bread, Fiesta Dip

Speedy Chili Dogs, Mexican Franks, Sloppy Joes, All-American Pizza Burgers

Easy Cheesy Bobolis, Hearty Stuffed Potatoes, Zesty Broccoli Slaw

Microwave Chili Dogs (page 79)

Easy Breakfast Treat

SERVES 6

Orange Juicy • Strawberry-French Toast Sandwiches • Bacon

Strawberry-French Toast Sandwiches

Strawberry-French Toast Sandwiches

¼ cup plus 2 tablespoons whipped cream cheese
12 slices sandwich bread
3 tablespoons strawberry jam
3 large eggs
3 tablespoons milk
⅛ teaspoon salt
2 to 3 tablespoons butter or margarine, divided
Powdered sugar
Garnish: strawberry fans

Spread 1 tablespoon cream cheese on each of six bread slices; spread 1½ teaspoons jam over cream cheese. Top with remaining slices of bread.

Combine eggs, milk, and salt in a shallow dish, beating well. Dip each sandwich into egg mixture, turning to coat both sides.

Melt 2 tablespoons butter in a large skillet; cook 3 sandwiches in butter until browned, turning to brown both sides. Repeat procedure with remaining sandwiches, adding more butter if necessary.

Sprinkle sandwiches with powdered sugar; serve immediately. Garnish, if desired. **Yield: 6 servings.**

Orange Juicy

1 (6-ounce) can frozen orange juice
    concentrate, undiluted
1 cup water
1 cup milk
¼ cup sugar
1 teaspoon vanilla extract
2 cups ice cubes

Combine all ingredients in container of an electric blender; process until smooth. Serve immediately. **Yield: 5 cups.**

TimeSavers

• Microwave bacon on a microwave-safe rack or paper plate. Cover bacon with paper towels; cook 6 slices at HIGH 5 minutes.

Fall Festival

(pictured on page 77)

SERVES 8

Microwave Chili Dogs • ◆ Kraut Relish
Corn chips • Oat 'n' Crunch Brownies

Microwave Chili Dogs

1 pound ground turkey
1 onion, chopped
1 green pepper, chopped (optional)
1 (15-ounce) can tomato sauce
2 tablespoons chili powder
½ teaspoon dried oregano
Dash of garlic powder
8 frankfurters, cooked
8 hot dog buns

Combine turkey, onion, and, if desired, green pepper in a 2-quart casserole. Cover with wax paper, and microwave at HIGH 6 minutes, stirring after 3 minutes; drain. Add tomato sauce and next 3 ingredients, stirring well. Microwave at HIGH 10 minutes, stirring after 5 minutes.

Place frankfurters in hot dog buns. Spoon turkey mixture over frankfurters. **Yield: 8 servings.**

Kraut Relish

1 (16-ounce) jar sauerkraut, drained
½ cup finely chopped celery
½ cup finely chopped green pepper
½ cup finely chopped carrot
½ cup finely chopped onion
¼ cup sugar

Combine all ingredients; cover and chill 8 hours. Serve relish with hot dogs, vegetables, or meats. **Yield: 1 quart.**

Oat 'n' Crunch Brownies

1 (21.5-ounce) package fudge brownie mix
½ cup chopped pecans
⅓ cup quick-cooking oats, uncooked
¼ cup firmly packed brown sugar
¼ teaspoon ground cinnamon (optional)
2 tablespoons butter or margarine, melted
¾ cup candy-coated chocolate pieces

Grease bottom of a 13- x 9- x 2-inch pan. Prepare brownie mix according to package directions; spoon into prepared pan.

Combine pecans, oats, brown sugar, and, if desired, cinnamon; stir in butter. Stir in candy; sprinkle over batter.

Bake at 350° for 35 minutes. Cool and cut into squares. **Yield: 3 dozen.**

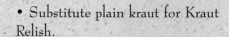

TimeSavers

• Substitute plain kraut for Kraut Relish.
• Bake brownies a day ahead.

Speedy Chili Dogs

Backyard Picnic

SERVES 8

Speedy Chili Dogs • ◆ Old-Fashioned Sweet Coleslaw
Potato chips • ◆ Lemon Ice Cream Tarts

Speedy Chili Dogs

1 pound ground beef
1 large onion, chopped
1 clove garlic, crushed
1 (16-ounce) can tomato sauce
¼ teaspoon salt
⅛ teaspoon pepper
1 to 2 tablespoons chili powder
1 cup water
8 frankfurters, cooked
8 hot dog buns, split and toasted
Shredded Cheddar cheese
Chopped green onions

Combine first 3 ingredients in a skillet; cook until beef is browned, stirring until it crumbles. Drain. Add tomato sauce and next 4 ingredients; cover, reduce heat, and simmer 25 minutes, stirring occasionally.

Place frankfurters in hot dog buns. Spoon chili mixture over frankfurters; top with cheese and green onions. **Yield: 8 servings.**

Old-Fashioned Sweet Coleslaw

5 cups finely chopped cabbage (about 1 small head)
2 carrots, scraped and shredded
1 to 2 tablespoons sugar
½ teaspoon salt
¼ teaspoon pepper
⅓ cup mayonnaise or salad dressing

Combine cabbage and carrot in a large bowl. Sprinkle with sugar, salt, and pepper; toss gently. Stir in mayonnaise. Cover and chill thoroughly. **Yield: 8 servings.**

Lemon Ice Cream Tarts

1 quart vanilla ice cream, slightly softened
1 (6-ounce) can frozen lemonade concentrate, undiluted
12 (3-inch) commercial graham cracker tart shells

Place softened ice cream and lemonade concentrate in container of an electric blender; process until smooth. Pour mixture into tart shells.

Place tart shells on a baking sheet, and freeze until firm. Place frozen tarts in heavy-duty, zip-top plastic bags. Carefully remove filled crusts about 5 minutes before serving. **Yield: 12 (3-inch) tarts.**

TimeSavers

• Select a packaged slaw mix that has shredded carrot in it.
• Make tarts in advance and freeze.

Kids' Company Supper

SERVES 10

Mexican Franks • Baked beans
Corn chips with Fiesta Dip • ◆ Frozen Cookie Crunch

Mexican Franks

10 (6-inch) corn tortillas
Vegetable oil
1 (15-ounce) can chili without beans
1 (8-ounce) can tomato sauce, divided
1 tablespoon minced onion
¼ teaspoon hot sauce
10 frankfurters
1 (4.5-ounce) can chopped green chiles, drained
1 cup (4 ounces) shredded Cheddar cheese

Fry tortillas, one at a time, in ¼-inch hot oil 3 to 5 seconds on each side or just until softened. Drain on paper towels. Set aside.

Combine chili, ¼ cup tomato sauce, onion, and hot sauce in a small bowl. Place a frankfurter in center of each tortilla; top each with 2 tablespoons chili mixture. Roll up, and place seam side down in a lightly greased 11- x 7- x 1½-inch baking dish. Combine remaining tomato sauce and remaining chili mixture; pour over tortillas.

Sprinkle with chiles. Cover and bake at 350° for 20 to 25 minutes. Uncover and sprinkle evenly with cheese; bake 5 additional minutes. **Yield: 10 servings.**

Fiesta Dip

1 (8-ounce) package cream cheese, softened
1 (8-ounce) jar mild picante sauce
Garnish: sliced green onions

Combine cream cheese and picante sauce; beat mixture at low speed of an electric mixer until smooth. Spoon into a small bowl, and garnish, if desired. Serve with corn chips or tortillas. **Yield: 2 cups.**

Frozen Cookie Crunch

1 (20-ounce) package cream-filled chocolate sandwich cookies, crushed
½ cup butter or margarine, melted
1 cup chopped pecans
½ gallon vanilla ice cream, softened

Combine first 3 ingredients. Pat one-third of cookie mixture in bottom of a lightly greased 13- x 9- x 2-inch pan; spread half of ice cream on top. Repeat procedure; sprinkle remaining crumbs on top. Freeze 8 hours. **Yield: 15 servings.**

TimeSavers

• Line your baking dishes or pans with aluminum foil for easy cleanup. Grease the foil if the recipe calls for this procedure.
• Soften cream cheese for dip in the microwave. Remove wrapper, place on a microwave-safe plate, and microwave at MEDIUM (50% power) 1 minute.
• Make dessert ahead and freeze.

Mexican Franks

Sloppy Joes and Jiffy Beans and Franks

Fourth of July Celebration

SERVES 6

Sloppy Joes • Jiffy Beans and Franks • Potato chips
Dill pickle spears • Root Beer Floats or watermelon slices

Sloppy Joes

1½ pounds ground beef
1 small onion, chopped
1 small green pepper, chopped
1 (10¾-ounce) can tomato soup
1 (8-ounce) can tomato sauce
2 tablespoons brown sugar (optional)
1 tablespoon Worcestershire sauce
1 teaspoon prepared mustard
Pinch of garlic powder
6 hamburger buns, split and toasted

Cook ground beef, onion, and green pepper in a large skillet until beef is browned, stirring to crumble; drain.

Stir in tomato soup and next 5 ingredients; simmer 10 to 15 minutes, stirring mixture often. Serve on toasted buns. **Yield: 6 servings.**

Jiffy Beans and Franks

2 (16-ounce) cans pork and beans
½ cup chopped onion
½ cup ketchup
¼ cup firmly packed brown sugar
½ teaspoon dry mustard
4 frankfurters, cut into ⅜-inch slices

Combine first 5 ingredients; spoon into a lightly greased, shallow 2-quart casserole. Cover with heavy-duty plastic wrap; fold back a small edge of wrap to allow steam to escape.

Microwave at HIGH 8 to 9 minutes, stirring once. Add frankfurters. Microwave at HIGH 8 to 9 minutes, stirring once. **Yield: 6 servings.**

Root Beer Floats

1 (1-liter) bottle root beer or other cola, divided
1 quart vanilla ice cream

Pour ½ cup root beer into each of 6 (12-ounce) soda glasses; spoon ice cream equally into glasses. Top each with remaining root beer. **Yield: 6 servings.**

TimeSavers

• Microwave Jiffy Beans and Franks while Sloppy Joe mixture is simmering.
• Allow ice cream time to soften before scooping, or peel away the carton and cut into slices with an electric knife.

All-American Pizza Burgers

1½ pounds lean ground beef
1½ pounds ground turkey sausage
Vegetable cooking spray
1 (14-ounce) jar pizza sauce, divided
¾ cup grated Parmesan cheese
1 medium onion, chopped (optional)
12 hamburger buns
12 slices mozzarella cheese

Combine ground beef and sausage; shape into 12 patties. Coat grill rack with cooking spray; place on grill over medium-hot coals (350° to 400°).

Place patties on rack, and cook, uncovered, 5 minutes on each side or until done, brushing patties occasionally with ¾ cup pizza sauce. (Discard any remaining pizza sauce used for brushing patties.)

Sprinkle with Parmesan cheese and, if desired, onion. Serve on buns with mozzarella cheese and remaining pizza sauce. **Yield: 12 servings.**

TimeSavers

• Shape ground meat into ½-inch-thick patties (¼ pound each), and stack between sheets of wax paper. If making patties ahead to freeze, place 2 pieces of wax paper between each patty, and place in a freezer bag.

• Preheat gas grill 20 minutes, or light charcoal 30 minutes before grilling burgers.

Ranch-Style Dip

¾ cup low-fat cottage cheese
1 (8-ounce) carton sour cream
1 cup mayonnaise or salad dressing
1 (1-ounce) envelope Ranch-style dressing mix

Place cottage cheese in container of an electric blender or food processor; process until smooth. Add sour cream and remaining ingredients; process until blended, stopping once to scrape down sides. Serve dip with fresh vegetables. **Yield: 2½ cups.**

Easy Chocolate Sauce

1 (14-ounce) can sweetened condensed milk
2 (1-ounce) squares unsweetened chocolate
2 tablespoons butter or margarine
Dash of salt
½ teaspoon vanilla extract

Combine all ingredients in a heavy saucepan; cook over low heat, stirring constantly with a wire whisk, until chocolate melts and mixture is smooth. Serve warm sauce over ice cream. **Yield: 1⅝ cups.**

All-American Pizza Burgers and Ranch-Style Dip with Vegetables

Easy Cheesy Bobolis and Santa's Hats

Saint Nick Party

SERVES 8

Easy Cheesy Bobolis

◆ Carrot and celery sticks with Christmas Confetti Dip • Santa's Hats

Easy Cheesy Bobolis

8 (6-inch) Bobolis
1 (14-ounce) jar pizza sauce
1 (3½-ounce) package pepperoni slices
1 (8-ounce) package shredded mozzarella
   cheese

Place Bobolis on ungreased baking sheets.
Spread pizza sauce evenly over Bobolis. Top
evenly with pepperoni slices, and sprinkle evenly
with cheese.
Bake at 350° for 15 minutes or until cheese
melts and Bobolis are thoroughly heated. **Yield:
8 servings.**

Christmas Confetti Dip

⅔ cup sour cream
⅓ cup mayonnaise or salad dressing
1 (2-ounce) jar diced pimiento, drained
2 tablespoons finely chopped chives
1 tablespoon finely chopped onion
¼ teaspoon garlic powder

Combine all ingredients; cover and chill up to
2 days. Serve with carrot and celery sticks.
Yield: about 1¼ cups.

Santa's Hats

½ gallon cherry-vanilla ice cream
1 (1-liter) bottle ginger ale
1 (8.75-ounce) can refrigerated instant
   whipped cream
Red decorator sugar crystals
8 maraschino cherries with stems

Divide ice cream evenly among 8 mugs or
glasses; pour ½ cup ginger ale over each. Top
each with whipped cream, sugar crystals, and
cherry. **Yield: 8 servings.**

TimeSavers

• Bobolis are baked pizza crusts
available in the deli section of most
supermarkets. Eight (6-inch) pita
bread rounds may be substituted.
• To save time, substitute a commercial dip for the Christmas
Confetti Dip, and purchase pre-cut
celery and carrot sticks.
• Canned instant whipped cream
magically becomes a "furry, white
hat" on Santa's Hats.

Hearty Stuffed Potatoes

School Night Fare

SERVES 4

Hearty Stuffed Potatoes • Bacon-Cheese French Bread
Old-Fashioned Strawberry Sodas

Hearty Stuffed Potatoes

4 large potatoes (about 2 pounds)
1 cup chopped fresh or frozen broccoli
1 small onion, chopped
1 cup chopped cooked ham or turkey
1 (2-ounce) jar diced pimiento, drained
Yogurt Sauce

Rinse potatoes, and pat dry. Prick each several times with a fork. Arrange in a circle, 1 inch apart, on a layer of paper towels in microwave oven.

Microwave, uncovered, at HIGH 14 to 17 minutes, turning and rearranging potatoes halfway through cooking time. Let stand 5 minutes.

Place broccoli and onion in a 1-quart glass bowl. Cover with heavy-duty plastic wrap; fold back a small edge of wrap to allow steam to escape. Microwave at HIGH 4 minutes or until tender. Drain.

Add ham and pimiento, and microwave at HIGH 2 to 3 minutes. Stir in Yogurt Sauce, and microwave at MEDIUM (50% power) 2 to 4 minutes or until mixture is thoroughly heated. (Do not boil.) Cut potatoes lengthwise, and top with yogurt mixture. **Yield: 4 servings.**

Yogurt Sauce

1 (8-ounce) carton plain low-fat yogurt
¼ cup mayonnaise or salad dressing
1 tablespoon tarragon vinegar
2 teaspoons cornstarch
1 teaspoon soy sauce
½ teaspoon dried thyme
½ teaspoon dry mustard
¼ teaspoon dried oregano
⅛ teaspoon garlic powder

Combine all ingredients, stirring until blended. **Yield: 1¼ cups.**

Bacon-Cheese French Bread

1 (16-ounce) loaf unsliced French bread, cut into 1-inch-thick slices
5 slices bacon, cooked and crumbled
1 (8-ounce) package shredded mozzarella cheese
¼ cup butter or margarine, melted

Place sliced loaf on aluminum foil. Combine bacon and cheese; place between bread slices. Drizzle with butter, and wrap in foil.

Bake at 350° for 20 minutes or until thoroughly heated. **Yield: 8 servings.**

Old-Fashioned Strawberry Sodas

1 (10-ounce) package frozen strawberries in syrup, thawed
3 cups strawberry ice cream, divided
2 (12-ounce) cans cream soda, divided
Garnish: whipped cream

Mash thawed strawberries with a fork until strawberries are well blended with syrup. Add 1 cup ice cream and ½ cup cream soda; stir well.

Spoon an equal amount of strawberry mixture into 4 (14-ounce) soda glasses; top with remaining ice cream, and fill glasses with remaining soda. Garnish, if desired. **Yield: 4 servings.**

Shrimp Basket Special

Gulf Coast Fried Shrimp

4 large eggs, beaten
⅔ cup commercial spicy French dressing
1½ tablespoons lemon juice
¾ teaspoon onion powder
2 pounds peeled, medium-size fresh shrimp
1⅓ cups saltine cracker crumbs
⅓ cup white cornmeal
⅔ cup crushed corn flakes cereal
Vegetable oil
Commercial cocktail sauce

   Combine first 4 ingredients; pour over shrimp. Stir gently; cover and chill 3 hours.
   Combine cracker crumbs, cornmeal, and crushed corn flakes. Remove shrimp from marinade; discard marinade. Dredge shrimp in crumb mixture.
   Pour oil to a depth of 2 to 3 inches in a Dutch oven; heat to 375°. Fry shrimp in hot oil until golden. Serve with cocktail sauce. **Yield: 6 servings.**

TimeSavers

• Commercial corn flake crumbs and cracker meal can be used to dredge shrimp. For easy cleanup, dredge shrimp in a plastic bag.
• Purchase frozen corn on the cob if fresh corn is unavailable.
• Substitute any type of 16-ounce package slaw mix for slaw.

Corn on the Cob with Herb Butter

¼ cup butter or margarine, softened
1 tablespoon chopped fresh parsley
1 tablespoon chopped fresh chives
¼ teaspoon dried salad herbs
About 2 quarts water
6 ears fresh corn

   Combine first 4 ingredients; set aside.
   Bring water to a boil, and add corn. Return to a boil, and cook 8 to 10 minutes. Drain well. Spread butter mixture over hot corn. **Yield: 6 servings.**

Zesty Broccoli Slaw

½ cup cider vinegar
½ cup vegetable oil
1 clove garlic, pressed
1½ teaspoons dried dillweed
½ teaspoon salt
1 (16-ounce) package fresh broccoli, carrot, and red cabbage slaw mix

   Combine first 5 ingredients; pour over slaw mix, stirring gently to coat.
   Cover and chill at least 2 hours. Drain slaw mix before serving, or serve with a slotted spoon. **Yield: 6 servings.**

Gulf Coast Fried Shrimp

Big Veggie Sandwich

1 (16-ounce) loaf unsliced whole wheat bread
1 (8-ounce) container chives-and-onion-
   flavored cream cheese
6 lettuce leaves
1 small green pepper, thinly sliced
1 large tomato, thinly sliced
2 avocados, peeled and sliced
1 small cucumber, thinly sliced
¾ cup alfalfa sprouts
¼ to ⅓ cup commercial Italian salad
   dressing

Cut bread into 12 slices, cutting to within ½ inch of bottom crust. Starting at first cut, carefully spread a thin layer of cream cheese on facing sides of both pieces of bread. Repeat procedure with every other cut.

Pull cheese-spread bread slices apart. Place a lettuce leaf between each sandwich and fill equally with vegetables. Drizzle Italian salad dressing into each sandwich. Serve sandwiches immediately, separating at unfilled cuts. **Yield: 6 servings.**

Big Veggie Sandwich

Combine first 5 ingredients in a saucepan. Cook over medium heat, stirring occasionally, until thoroughly heated. Sprinkle each serving with crumbled bacon and green onions. **Yield: 1 quart.**

Corn Chowder

1 (10¾-ounce) can cream of potato soup
1 (17-ounce) can reduced-sodium whole
   kernel corn, drained
1⅓ cups milk
1 tablespoon butter or margarine
½ teaspoon pepper
4 slices bacon, cooked and crumbled
2 small green onions, sliced

TimeSavers

• Save time by making 1 large sandwich and cutting it into 6 servings. The thinner you slice the vegetables, the easier it is to keep the sandwich together.
• Substitute bacon bits for crumbled bacon if you don't have a supply of cooked bacon in the freezer.

Breakfast and Brunch

Serve an omelet for a festive morning treat, or quickly exit the kitchen during the week with other fast-to-fix breakfast menus. Then make a leisurely brunch the highlight of your weekend.

Ambrosia Pancakes with Orange Syrup, Lightnin' Cheese Biscuits

Apple Breakfast Sandwiches, Shrimp-and-Egg Salad Sandwiches, Crabmeat Salad

Easy Mexican Omelet, Shrimp-and-Cheese Omelet, Marmalade Breakfast Pears

Quick Eggs Benedict, Club Soda Waffles, Herbed Cheese Omelet

Easy Pancakes (page 101)

Herbed Cheese Omelet

Lazy Morning Breakfast

SERVES 4

Herbed Cheese Omelet • ◆ Fresh fruit with Sour Cream Sauce • Quick Biscuits

Herbed Cheese Omelet

1 (3-ounce) package cream cheese, softened
1½ teaspoons sour cream
¼ teaspoon lemon juice
¼ teaspoon dried parsley flakes
⅛ teaspoon salt
⅛ teaspoon garlic powder
⅛ teaspoon ground white pepper
⅛ teaspoon dried dillweed
8 large eggs
2 tablespoons water
½ teaspoon ground white pepper
1 tablespoon olive oil
1 tablespoon butter or margarine
2 tablespoons chopped green onions

Combine first 3 ingredients in a large bowl; add parsley flakes and next 4 ingredients, mixing well.

Combine eggs, water, and ½ teaspoon white pepper; stir with a wire whisk or fork until blended.

Heat a heavy 10-inch skillet over medium heat until hot enough to sizzle a drop of water. Add olive oil and butter, and rotate skillet to coat bottom. Pour egg mixture into skillet. As mixture starts to cook, gently lift edges of omelet with a spatula, and tilt skillet so uncooked portion flows underneath.

Spoon cream cheese mixture in center of omelet, and fold sides over filling. Sprinkle with green onions, and serve immediately. **Yield: 4 servings.**

Sour Cream Sauce

¾ cup sour cream
2 tablespoons orange juice concentrate, thawed and undiluted
3 tablespoons honey

Combine all ingredients; cover and chill. Serve over fresh fruit. **Yield: 1 cup.**

Quick Biscuits

2 cups self-rising flour
⅔ cup buttermilk
⅓ cup corn oil

Combine all ingredients in a medium bowl, stirring just until dry ingredients are moistened. Turn dough out onto a floured surface, and knead dough 3 or 4 times.

Roll dough to ½-inch thickness; cut with a 2-inch biscuit cutter. Place biscuits on an ungreased baking sheet.

Bake at 425° for 10 to 12 minutes or until biscuits are golden. **Yield: 1 dozen.**

Note: Mix up a powdered buttermilk blend if you don't have fresh buttermilk on hand.

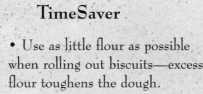

TimeSaver

• Use as little flour as possible when rolling out biscuits—excess flour toughens the dough.

Easy Mexican Omelet

Zippy Omelet Brunch

SERVES 2

Easy Mexican Omelet • Hash Brown Potatoes
Crusty Broiled Tomatoes • English muffins

Easy Mexican Omelet

3 large eggs
½ teaspoon salt
¼ teaspoon pepper
1 tablespoon water
1 tablespoon butter or margarine
¾ cup (3 ounces) shredded Monterey Jack
  cheese
2 tablespoons sliced jalapeño peppers
2 tablespoons salsa

Combine first 4 ingredients; stir with a wire whisk just until blended.

Heat a heavy 8-inch skillet over medium heat until hot enough to sizzle a drop of water. Add butter, and rotate skillet to coat bottom.

Pour egg mixture into skillet; sprinkle with cheese and jalapeño peppers. As mixture starts to cook, gently lift edges of omelet with a spatula, and tilt skillet so that uncooked portion flows underneath. Fold omelet in half, and transfer to plate. Top with salsa. **Yield: 2 servings.**

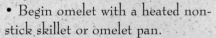

TimeSavers

• Begin omelet with a heated non-stick skillet or omelet pan.
• Use leftover cooked potatoes, or cut potatoes into small pieces to cook faster.
• Cut a thin slice off bottom of tomatoes to help them sit flat. Assemble tomatoes ahead and chill, if desired.

Hash Brown Potatoes

1 tablespoon bacon drippings
1 tablespoon butter or margarine
2 cups diced cooked potato
⅓ cup minced onion
1 tablespoon minced fresh parsley
1 clove garlic, minced
Salt and pepper to taste

Melt bacon drippings and butter in a heavy 9-inch skillet. Add remaining ingredients, stirring gently until coated. Cook mixture, uncovered, 15 to 20 minutes or until browned on all sides, turning occasionally. **Yield: 2 servings.**

Crusty Broiled Tomatoes

2 small tomatoes
2 teaspoons Dijon mustard
Dash of salt and black pepper
Dash of ground red pepper
3 tablespoons butter or margarine, melted
¼ cup dry breadcrumbs
¼ cup grated Parmesan cheese

Cut tomatoes in half crosswise. Spread cut side with mustard; sprinkle with salt, pepper, and red pepper.

Combine butter, breadcrumbs, and cheese; spoon evenly over tomato halves. Broil 5½ inches from heat (with electric oven door partially open) 2 to 4 minutes or until lightly browned. Serve immediately. **Yield: 2 servings.**

Sunday Morning Special

SERVES 2

Shrimp-and-Cheese Omelet • Fruit cup
Easy Herb Biscuits • Bloody Marys

Shrimp-and-Cheese Omelet

Shrimp-and-Cheese Omelet

4 large eggs
2 tablespoons water
2 tablespoons butter or margarine, divided
⅓ cup (1.3 ounces) shredded Monterey Jack
cheese
½ cup coarsely chopped cooked shrimp
2 tablespoons sliced green onions
1 tablespoon chopped fresh parsley
Garnishes: whole shrimp, green onions

Whisk together eggs and water; set aside.

Heat an 8-inch omelet pan or nonstick skillet over medium heat. Add 1 tablespoon butter, and rotate pan to coat.

Add half of egg mixture. As mixture starts to cook, gently lift edges of omelet with a spatula, and tilt pan so that uncooked portion of omelet flows underneath.

Sprinkle half of omelet with half each of cheese and next 3 ingredients; fold omelet in half. Transfer to a serving plate. Repeat procedure with remaining egg and filling mixtures. Garnish, if desired. Serve immediately. **Yield: 2 servings.**

Easy Herb Biscuits

2 cups biscuit mix
1 tablespoon freeze-dried chives
1 teaspoon dried parsley flakes
¾ cup plain yogurt

Combine all ingredients in a medium bowl, stirring just until dry ingredients are moistened. Turn dough out onto a floured surface, and knead lightly 4 or 5 times.

Roll dough to ½-inch thickness; cut with a 2½-inch biscuit cutter. Place biscuits on a lightly greased baking sheet. Bake at 450° for 8 minutes or until lightly browned. **Yield: 6 biscuits.**

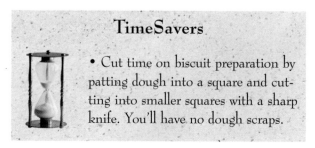

TimeSavers

• Cut time on biscuit preparation by patting dough into a square and cutting into smaller squares with a sharp knife. You'll have no dough scraps.

Favorite Family Breakfast
(pictured on page 95)
SERVES 4
Easy Pancakes • Cranberry-Apple Sauce
Baked Sausage Patties • Orange juice

Easy Pancakes

2½ cups biscuit mix
2 large eggs, beaten
1⅓ cups milk
2 tablespoons vegetable oil

Place biscuit mix in a medium bowl; make a well in center. Combine eggs, milk, and oil; add to biscuit mix, stirring just until dry ingredients are moistened.

Pour about ¼ cup batter for each pancake onto a moderately hot, lightly greased griddle. Turn pancakes when tops are covered with bubbles and edges of pancakes look cooked. **Yield: 16 pancakes.**

Cranberry-Apple Sauce

1 (16-ounce) can whole-berry cranberry sauce
2 small cooking apples, cored and chopped
⅓ cup apple juice

Combine all ingredients in a small saucepan; bring to a boil, stirring constantly. Reduce heat and simmer, stirring occasionally, 6 minutes or until apples are tender.

Serve warm over pancakes. Store sauce in refrigerator. **Yield: 2½ cups.**

Baked Sausage Patties

1 pound ground pork sausage

Shape sausage into 8 patties about ¾-inch thick; place on a rack in a broiler pan. Bake at 375° for 15 to 20 minutes or until done. Drain on paper towels. **Yield: 8 servings.**

To make ahead: Prepare as directed; let cool. Wrap in aluminum foil; chill. Bake at 350° in foil 10 minutes or until thoroughly heated.

TimeSavers

• Stir pancake batter only until dry ingredients are moistened— batter will still be lumpy. Beating batter until smooth produces tough pancakes.
• Save time by using a wide-mouth pitcher to mix and pour pancake batter.
• Make sausage patties and sauce for pancakes ahead of time.

Wake Up to Pancakes

SERVES 4

Ambrosia Pancakes with Orange Syrup • Crisp bacon
Summer Fruit Bowl • Milk

Ambrosia Pancakes with Orange Syrup

Ambrosia Pancakes with Orange Syrup

1 large egg, beaten
1 cup milk
½ cup flaked coconut
1 tablespoon vegetable oil
1 teaspoon grated orange rind
1 cup pancake-and-waffle mix
Orange Syrup

Combine first 5 ingredients, stirring well. Add pancake mix; stir just until dry ingredients are moistened.

Pour about 2 tablespoons batter for each pancake onto a hot, lightly greased griddle. Turn pancakes when tops are covered with bubbles and edges look cooked. Serve with Orange Syrup. **Yield: 12 pancakes.**

Orange Syrup

1 cup orange sections, coarsely chopped
1 cup maple-flavored syrup

Combine ingredients in a small saucepan. Cook until thoroughly heated. **Yield: 1½ cups.**

Summer Fruit Bowl

1½ cups cubed cantaloupe
1 cup sliced fresh strawberries
1 cup cubed fresh pineapple
⅓ cup fresh blueberries

Combine all fruit; toss gently. **Yield: 4 servings.**

TimeSavers

• Use a nonstick griddle or skillet for pancakes. The griddle is hot enough when a drop of water sizzles on it.
• Buy cored, peeled pineapple and cubed cantaloupe from the produce section of your supermarket.

Easy Waffle Breakfast

SERVES 6

Club Soda Waffles • Maple syrup • Bacon or sausage
◆ Colorful Fruit Bowl • Sparkling Apple Juice • Milk

Club Soda Waffles

2¼ cups biscuit mix
3 tablespoons vegetable oil
1 large egg
1 (10-ounce) bottle club soda
Garnish: fresh strawberries

Combine first 3 ingredients in a large mixing bowl; stir until blended. Add club soda; beat at medium speed of an electric mixer until blended.

Bake in a preheated, oiled waffle iron until golden. Garnish, if desired, and serve with maple syrup. **Yield: 14 (4-inch) waffles.**

Club Soda Waffles

Colorful Fruit Bowl

1 (8-ounce) carton plain yogurt
1 tablespoon sugar
1 teaspoon lemon juice
1 cup orange sections, chilled
1 cup grapefruit sections, chilled
1 medium banana, sliced
1 cup sliced strawberries
1 cup cubed honeydew melon

Combine first 3 ingredients; chill. Combine orange sections and remaining fruit, tossing gently.

Drizzle yogurt dressing over each serving; serve immediately. **Yield: 6 servings.**

Sparkling Apple Juice

1 (12-ounce) can frozen apple juice
    concentrate, thawed and undiluted
1 (23-ounce) bottle sparkling mineral water,
    chilled

Combine ingredients; stir gently. Serve immediately over crushed ice. **Yield: about 4½ cups.**

TimeSavers

• Use club soda at room temperature to make waffles extra light. Bake waffles immediately.
• Make a double batch of waffles and freeze leftovers; reheat in a toaster or toaster oven.

Out-of-the-Ordinary Breakfast
SERVES 10
Apple Breakfast Sandwiches • Link sausage
♦ Fruit Cup with Rum • Perky Cranberry Punch • Orange juice

Apple Breakfast Sandwiches

⅓ cup firmly packed brown sugar
2 tablespoons all-purpose flour
½ teaspoon ground cinnamon
1 (10-ounce) can refrigerated buttermilk
    biscuits
1 cup (4 ounces) shredded sharp Cheddar
    cheese
2 large apples, peeled, cored, and cut into
    rings
1 tablespoon butter or margarine, melted

Combine first 3 ingredients in a small bowl;
set aside.

Separate biscuits, and press each into a 3-inch
circle. Place on lightly greased baking sheets;
sprinkle with cheese, and top each with an apple
ring. Sprinkle with reserved sugar mixture, and
drizzle with butter.

Bake at 350° for 15 minutes or until crust is
golden. Serve immediately. **Yield: 10 servings.**

TimeSavers

• Get a head start on your weekend
breakfast by fixing the fruit cup the
night before.
• Cook link sausage while sandwiches bake.

Fruit Cup with Rum

1 (17-ounce) can apricot halves, drained
1 (16-ounce) can sliced peaches, drained
1 (16-ounce) can sliced pears, drained
1 (15¼-ounce) can pineapple chunks, drained
1 (11-ounce) can mandarin oranges, drained
½ cup rum

Combine fruit in a large bowl; add rum, and
toss gently. Cover and chill 8 hours. **Yield: 12
servings.**

Perky Cranberry Punch

2 (32-ounce) bottles cranberry juice
1 (46-ounce) can unsweetened pineapple juice
2 cups water
1 cup firmly packed brown sugar
2 tablespoons whole allspice
2 tablespoons whole cloves
6 (3-inch) sticks cinnamon

Pour first 3 ingredients into a large percolator.
Place brown sugar and remaining ingredients in
percolator basket.

Perk through complete cycle of electric percolator. **Yield: 1 gallon.**

Apple Breakfast Sandwiches

Quick Eggs Benedict

Weekend Eye-Opener

SERVES 6

Quick Eggs Benedict • Cherry tomatoes
Grapefruit in Champagne • Spiced-Up Coffee • Orange juice

Quick Eggs Benedict

6 slices Canadian bacon
1 (11-ounce) can Cheddar cheese soup
2 tablespoons milk
3 tablespoons dry sherry
6 large eggs
3 English muffins, split and toasted
Paprika

Cook bacon over medium heat 3 minutes on each side. Set aside.

Combine soup and milk in a small saucepan; cook over medium heat, stirring until blended. Stir in sherry; reduce heat to low.

Pour water to a depth of 2 inches into a lightly greased deep skillet. Bring water to a boil; reduce heat, and maintain at a light simmer. Break eggs, one at a time, into a saucer. Slip eggs, one at a time, into water, holding saucer as close as possible to surface of water. Simmer 3 to 5 minutes or to desired degree of doneness. Remove eggs with a slotted spoon. Drain eggs on paper towels. Trim edges of eggs, if desired.

Place a slice of Canadian bacon on each toasted muffin half; top with a poached egg, and cover with cheese sauce. Sprinkle with paprika. **Yield: 6 servings.**

Grapefruit in Champagne

4 cups grapefruit sections, chilled
1 cup pink champagne, chilled
Garnish: fresh mint leaves

Combine grapefruit sections and champagne; spoon into 6 stemmed glasses; garnish, if desired. **Yield: 6 servings.**

Spiced-Up Coffee

⅔ cup ground coffee
1 teaspoon vanilla extract
1 teaspoon almond extract
6 cups water

Place coffee in coffee filter or filter basket; spoon flavorings over coffee.

Add water to coffeemaker, and brew. Serve immediately. **Yield: about 6 cups.**

TimeSavers

• A soup-based sauce replaces classic Hollandaise sauce in the entrée.
• Use an egg ring or a clean tuna can (top and bottom removed) to hold the shape of eggs while poaching. Oil the ring before using.
• Purchase refrigerated grapefruit sections.

Anyday Brunch

SERVES 6

Shrimp-and-Egg Salad Sandwiches

Marmalade Breakfast Pears • Mimosas

Shrimp-and-Egg Salad Sandwiches

Shrimp-and-Egg Salad Sandwiches

½ pound peeled, medium-size cooked shrimp,
    coarsely chopped
6 large hard-cooked eggs, chopped
¼ cup finely chopped green onions
2 tablespoons finely chopped celery
1 tablespoon chopped fresh parsley
2 tablespoons capers (optional)
2 teaspoons chopped fresh dill (optional)
3 tablespoons mayonnaise or salad dressing
1 teaspoon lemon juice
1 teaspoon prepared mustard
¼ teaspoon salt
¼ teaspoon hot sauce
Leaf lettuce
3 English muffins, split and toasted
Garnishes: fresh dill, whole shrimp,
    lemon slices

Combine first 5 ingredients; stir in capers and dill, if desired. Set aside.

Combine mayonnaise and next 4 ingredients, and gently fold into egg mixture.

Place lettuce on English muffin halves; spoon egg mixture over lettuce. Garnish, if desired. **Yield: 6 servings.**

Marmalade Breakfast Pears

⅓ cup orange marmalade
¼ cup orange juice
2 (16-ounce) cans pear halves, drained
½ cup sour cream
2 teaspoons grated orange rind
½ teaspoon ground cinnamon

Combine marmalade and orange juice in an 8-inch square baking dish. Arrange pears, cut side down, in dish. Cover and microwave at HIGH 4 to 5 minutes or until pears are hot. Let stand 2 minutes, basting pears occasionally with juice mixture.

Spoon pears and juice into individual bowls.

Combine sour cream, orange rind, and cinnamon, stirring well. Serve over pears. **Yield: 6 servings.**

Mimosas

1 (750-milliliter) bottle champagne, chilled
1 (6-ounce) can frozen orange juice
    concentrate, thawed and diluted

Combine chilled champagne and orange juice just before serving. **Yield: 1½ quarts.**

TimeSavers

• Cooked pear mixture may be chilled overnight and served cold.
• Cook eggs in advance. To keep egg shells from cracking when hard-cooking eggs, pierce the large end with an egg piercer. The eggs will also be easier to peel.
• Thaw orange juice concentrate in microwave or overnight in refrigerator.

Summertime Brunch

SERVES 4

◆ Crabmeat Salad • Lightnin' Cheese Biscuits • Sunshine Fizz

Crabmeat Salad

1 dozen fresh asparagus spears
⅓ cup sour cream
⅓ cup mayonnaise or salad dressing
2 teaspoons Dijon mustard
2 teaspoons white wine vinegar
½ teaspoon dried tarragon
¼ teaspoon dried basil
1 tablespoon chopped green onions
½ teaspoon prepared horseradish
4 cups shredded lettuce
1 pound fresh lump crabmeat, drained
4 marinated artichoke hearts, halved
2 hard-cooked eggs, quartered
Garnish: pimiento strips

Snap off tough ends of asparagus. Arrange asparagus in a steaming rack, and place over boiling water. Cover and steam 5 minutes or until crisp-tender. Drain. Chill 1 hour.

Combine sour cream and next 7 ingredients in a small bowl. Line each of 4 individual salad plates with 1 cup lettuce.

Divide crabmeat among plates. Divide artichokes, asparagus, and hard-cooked eggs among plates, and arrange around crabmeat. Serve with dressing. Garnish, if desired. **Yield: 4 servings.**

Lightnin' Cheese Biscuits

2 cups biscuit mix
⅔ cup (2.6 ounces) finely shredded Cheddar
   cheese
½ cup water

Combine all ingredients in a medium bowl, stirring just until moistened. Turn dough out onto a well-floured surface, and knead 15 to 20 times.

Pat dough to ½-inch thickness; cut with a 2½-inch biscuit cutter. Place biscuits on a lightly greased baking sheet. Bake at 450° for 8 to 10 minutes or until lightly browned. **Yield: 1 dozen.**

Sunshine Fizz

1½ cups orange juice, chilled
1½ cups pineapple juice, chilled
1½ cups orange sherbet
¾ cup club soda, chilled
Orange sherbet

Combine first 3 ingredients in container of an electric blender; process until smooth. Stir in club soda, and pour into soda glasses. Add a scoop of orange sherbet to each glass. Serve immediately. **Yield: 4 servings.**

TimeSavers

• Steam asparagus and cook eggs a day ahead. Eggs that are one week old prior to hard-cooking are easier to peel than those that are less than one week old.
• Chill juices and club soda the night before.

Crabmeat Salad

Curried Chicken-Rice Salad

Late-Morning Brunch

SERVES 6

Curried Chicken-Rice Salad • Orange Broccoli
Sour Cream Muffins • Lemon Frappé

Curried Chicken-Rice Salad

3 cups chopped cooked chicken
1½ cups cooked rice
1 cup chopped celery
1 cup seedless green grapes, halved
½ cup chopped pecans, toasted
⅓ cup sweet pickle relish
¾ cup mayonnaise
1 teaspoon curry powder
½ teaspoon salt
¼ teaspoon pepper
Lettuce leaves
1 pint fresh strawberries
1 fresh pineapple, peeled and cut into spears

Combine first 6 ingredients in a medium bowl. Combine mayonnaise and next 3 ingredients; add to chicken mixture, stirring well.

Serve on lettuce leaves with strawberries and pineapple. **Yield: 6 servings.**

Orange Broccoli

1½ pounds broccoli spears
¼ cup butter or margarine, softened
1 tablespoon grated orange rind
2 tablespoons orange juice

Arrange broccoli in a steaming rack, and place over boiling water. Cover and steam 8 to 10 minutes or until tender. Place in a serving bowl.

Combine butter, orange rind, and orange juice in a small bowl. Top broccoli with butter mixture. **Yield: 6 servings.**

Sour Cream Muffins

½ cup butter, softened
1 (8-ounce) carton sour cream
2 cups biscuit mix

Cream butter; stir in sour cream. Gradually add biscuit mix, stirring just until moistened.

Spoon into lightly greased miniature muffin pans, filling two-thirds full. Bake at 350° for 15 minutes or until lightly browned. **Yield: 3 dozen.**

Note: Muffins can be made in regular muffin pans. Bake at 350° for 20 minutes. **Yield: 1 dozen.**

Lemon Frappé

1 (6-ounce) can frozen lemonade concentrate, undiluted
1½ cups water
1 pint lemon ice cream or sherbet
1 (12-ounce) can ginger ale

Combine first 3 ingredients in container of an electric blender; process until smooth. Spoon into pitcher; stir in ginger ale. **Yield: 5 cups.**

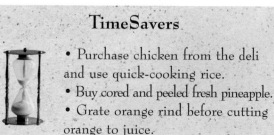

TimeSavers

• Purchase chicken from the deli and use quick-cooking rice.
• Buy cored and peeled fresh pineapple.
• Grate orange rind before cutting orange to juice.

Ham Roll Casserole

2 (10-ounce) packages frozen broccoli spears
8 (1-ounce) slices Swiss cheese
8 (6- x 4-inch) slices cooked ham
1 (10¾-ounce) can cream of mushroom soup, undiluted
½ cup sour cream
2 teaspoons Dijon mustard
2 tablespoons sliced almonds

Place broccoli in a 12- x 8- x 2-inch baking dish. Cover tightly with heavy-duty plastic wrap; fold back a small corner of wrap to allow steam to escape. Microwave at HIGH 2 to 3 minutes. Rearrange spears. Cover and microwave at HIGH 3 to 4 minutes. Drain broccoli; set aside.

Place 1 slice of cheese on each ham slice. Divide broccoli into 8 portions; arrange a portion on each ham slice, placing stems in the center and flowerets to the outside. Roll up securely, and place seam side down in greased 12-x 8- x 2-inch baking dish.

Combine soup, sour cream, and mustard; pour over ham rolls. Sprinkle with almonds. Cover with heavy-duty plastic wrap; fold back a small corner of wrap to allow steam to escape. Microwave at HIGH 8 to 10 minutes or until casserole is thoroughly heated, giving dish a half-turn after 5 minutes. **Yield: 4 to 6 servings.**

Conventional directions: Cook broccoli according to package directions. Assemble casserole; cover and bake at 350° for 20 minutes or until bubbly.

Whipping Cream Biscuits

1¾ cups all-purpose flour
2½ teaspoons baking powder
½ teaspoon salt
1 cup whipping cream

Combine flour, baking powder, and salt in a medium bowl; stir until well blended. Add whipping cream; stir with a fork just until moistened.

Turn dough out onto a lightly floured surface, and knead 4 or 5 times. Roll dough to ½-inch thickness; cut with a 2-inch biscuit cutter.

Place biscuits 1-inch apart on an ungreased baking sheet. Bake at 450° for 10 minutes or until lightly browned. Serve hot. **Yield: 1 dozen.**

Variations

Bacon Biscuits: Add ⅓ cup cooked crumbled bacon to dry ingredients.

Cheese Biscuits: Add ½ cup (2 ounces) shredded sharp Cheddar cheese to dry ingredients.

Herb Biscuits: Add 1¼ teaspoons caraway seeds, ½ teaspoon dried whole sage, and ¼ teaspoon dry mustard to dry ingredients.

Raspberry Kir

4 cups Chablis or other dry white wine, chilled
1½ tablespoons Chambord or other raspberry liqueur

Pour ⅔ cup wine in each wine glass.

Add ¾ teaspoon Chambord to each one, and stir well. **Yield: 6 servings.**

Ham Roll Casserole

Hearty Breakfast Fare
SERVES 4
Breakfast Pita Pockets • ◆ Yogurt-Granola Fruit Medley • Orange juice

Breakfast Pita Pockets

½ **pound ground pork sausage**
4 **large eggs**
¼ **cup milk**
½ **teaspoon dried oregano**
⅛ **to ¼ teaspoon salt**
¼ **teaspoon pepper**
4 **slices Provolone cheese (about 1 ounce each)**
4 **(6-inch) pita bread rounds**

Crumble sausage into a shallow 1-quart casserole. Cover tightly with heavy-duty plastic wrap; fold back a small edge of wrap to allow steam to escape. Microwave at HIGH 3 to 4 minutes or until sausage is browned, stirring once. Drain well on paper towels. Set aside.

Combine eggs and next 4 ingredients in shallow 1-quart casserole, mixing well. Microwave at HIGH 2 to 4 minutes, pushing cooked portion to center at 1-minute intervals.

Cut cheese and pita bread rounds in half. Line each bread half with one piece of cheese. Combine sausage and egg mixture; spoon about ¼ cup sausage-egg mixture into pita pockets.

Wrap each pita pocket in a paper towel. Place 4 pita pockets on a paper plate or glass pizza plate, and microwave at MEDIUM (50% power) 1 to 2 minutes or until warm. Repeat process with remaining sandwiches. **Yield: 4 servings.**

Breakfast Pita Pockets

Yogurt-Granola Fruit Medley

2 **bananas, sliced**
1 **(8-ounce) carton vanilla yogurt**
1 **cup granola**
2 **cups seedless grapes**

Layer half of banana slices in a 1-quart bowl; lightly spread one-fourth of yogurt on top, and sprinkle with one-fourth of granola.

Arrange half of grapes over granola; spread with one-fourth of yogurt, and sprinkle with one-fourth of granola.

Repeat procedure with remaining ingredients. Cover and chill up to 3 hours. **Yield: 4 servings.**

Company's Coming

Relax and celebrate simplicity with these menus. Whether you wish to host a cookout with panache or an elegant seated dinner, you'll find a quick and easy menu here.

Grilled Salmon Steaks, Pepper Steak Stir-Fry, Mediterranean Chicken

Easy Crab Imperial, Fiery Cajun Shrimp, Lime-Buttered Turkey Tenderloins

Honey-Gingered Pork Tenderloin, Pork Piccata, Lemon-Dill Chicken Sauté

Grouper with Sautéed Vegetables, Tuna Steaks with Tarragon Butter

Baked Chicken with Tarragon Sauce (page 128)

Stir Up a Stir-Fry

SERVES 4

Pepper Steak Stir-Fry • Fresh fruit with Tangy Sauce
Crusty rolls • ◆ Almond Ice Cream Balls

Pepper Steak Stir-Fry

1¼ pounds sirloin steak (1-inch thick)
1 tablespoon cornstarch
¼ cup water
½ cup canned diluted beef broth
¼ cup soy sauce
¼ cup vegetable oil
1 clove garlic, minced
1 teaspoon ground ginger
½ teaspoon salt
½ teaspoon pepper
1 large green pepper, cut into strips
1 large sweet red pepper, cut into strips
1 large onion, thinly sliced
1 (6-ounce) can sliced water chestnuts,
    drained
4 green onions, cut into 1-inch pieces
Hot cooked rice

Partially freeze steak; slice diagonally across the grain into 1½- x ⅛-inch strips. Set aside.

Combine cornstarch and water in a small bowl, stirring until smooth; add beef broth and soy sauce. Set aside.

Heat oil in a skillet over medium-high heat; add garlic, ginger, salt, and pepper, and cook 1 minute, stirring constantly. Add steak, and cook 2 minutes or until browned; remove from skillet. Add pepper strips and onion, and cook 3 minutes or until crisp-tender. Add beef, water chestnuts, green onions, and broth mixture; cook 2 minutes or until thickened. Serve over rice. **Yield: 4 servings.**

Tangy Sauce

⅓ cup frozen lemonade concentrate, thawed
⅓ cup vegetable oil
⅓ cup honey
1 teaspoon celery seeds

Combine all ingredients in container of an electric blender; blend 1 minute. Serve with fresh fruit. **Yield: 1 cup.**

Almond Ice Cream Balls

1 pint vanilla ice cream
1 (2-ounce) package slivered almonds,
    chopped and toasted
½ cup commercial fudge sauce
2 teaspoons amaretto or 1 teaspoon almond
    extract

Scoop ice cream into 4 balls, and place on a baking sheet; freeze at least 1 hour or until firm.

Coat ice cream balls with almonds; freeze.

Combine fudge sauce and amaretto. Place ice cream balls in dessert dishes; top with sauce. Serve immediately. **Yield: 4 servings.**

TimeSavers

• Peppers are easier to slice if you cut from the flesh (not the skin) side.
• Store individually wrapped almond-coated ice cream balls in a freezer bag or container for a quick dessert.

Pepper Steak Stir-Fry

Veal Piccata

A Little Dinner for Two

SERVES 2

Veal Piccata • Green Beans with Buttered Pecans
Sparkling Mushrooms • Whole-grain hard rolls • Lemon sherbet

Veal Piccata

4 veal cutlets (about ¾ pound)
¼ cup all-purpose flour
½ teaspoon salt
¼ teaspoon pepper
1½ tablespoons peanut or vegetable oil
3 tablespoons vermouth or dry white wine
2 tablespoons butter or margarine
2 tablespoons lemon juice
2 teaspoons grated lemon rind
Garnishes: lemon slices, parsley

Place cutlets between two sheets of heavy-duty plastic wrap; flatten to ⅛-inch thickness, using a meat mallet or rolling pin.

Combine flour, salt, and pepper; dredge cutlets in flour mixture. Cook in oil in a skillet over medium heat 1 minute on each side. Remove from skillet; keep warm.

Add vermouth to skillet; cook until thoroughly heated. Add butter and lemon juice; heat just until butter melts. Pour over cutlets, and sprinkle with lemon rind. Garnish, if desired. **Yield: 2 servings.**

TimeSavers

• Store veal in the coldest part of the refrigerator for no more than 2 days.
• Use a plastic bag for dredging veal to make cleanup a snap.
• Grate lemon rind while lemon is whole, and then cut lemon in half to juice.

Green Beans with Buttered Pecans

2 cups water
¼ teaspoon salt
½ pound trimmed green beans
1 tablespoon butter or margarine
2 tablespoons chopped pecans
⅛ teaspoon pepper

Bring water and salt to a boil in a medium saucepan. Add green beans; cook, uncovered, 10 minutes or just until crisp-tender. Drain beans, and set aside.

Melt butter in a nonstick skillet; add pecans, and cook until golden, stirring often. Add beans; toss gently, and cook until thoroughly heated. Sprinkle with pepper. **Yield: 2 servings.**

Sparkling Mushrooms

1 (8-ounce) carton small whole mushrooms
2 tablespoons olive oil
½ teaspoon dried rosemary
⅛ teaspoon salt
⅛ teaspoon pepper
½ cup champagne or sparkling wine

Cook mushrooms in olive oil in a large skillet over medium-high heat, stirring constantly, 1 to 2 minutes.

Add rosemary, salt, and pepper; cook 1 minute. Stir in champagne; reduce heat, and simmer 5 minutes. **Yield: 2 servings.**

Hot Off the Coals

SERVES 6

◆ Honey-Gingered Pork Tenderloin • Vegetable Kabobs
Garlic bread • ◆ Strawberries Jamaica

Honey-Gingered Pork Tenderloin

2 (¾-pound) pork tenderloins
¼ cup honey
¼ cup soy sauce
¼ cup oyster sauce
2 tablespoons brown sugar
1 tablespoon minced fresh gingerroot
1 tablespoon minced garlic
1 tablespoon ketchup
¼ teaspoon ground red pepper
¼ teaspoon ground cinnamon
Garnish: fresh parsley sprigs

Place tenderloins in an 11- x 7- x 1½-inch dish. Combine honey and next 8 ingredients, stirring well; pour over tenderloins. Cover and marinate in refrigerator 8 hours, turning occasionally.

Remove tenderloins from marinade; pour marinade into a saucepan, and bring to a boil.

Grill tenderloins, covered with grill lid, over medium-hot coals (350° to 400°) 15 minutes or until meat thermometer registers 160°, turning often and basting with reserved marinade.

Cut tenderloins into thin slices, and arrange on a serving platter. Garnish, if desired. **Yield: 6 servings.**

TimeSavers

• Look for pork tenderloin packaged in vacuum-sealed plastic bags at the meat counter.
• Purchase oyster sauce, a popular Oriental seasoning, at your local supermarket.

Vegetable Kabobs

3 medium onions, quartered
1 medium zucchini, cut into 1-inch slices
3 medium-size yellow squash, cut into 1-inch slices
12 medium fresh mushrooms
12 cherry tomatoes
¼ cup butter or margarine, melted
¼ teaspoon ground cumin

Arrange vegetables on 6 skewers. Combine butter and cumin; brush vegetables with butter mixture.

Grill kabobs, covered with grill lid, over medium-hot coals (350° to 400°) 10 to 15 minutes or until zucchini and yellow squash are crisp-tender, turning occasionally and brushing with butter mixture. **Yield: 6 servings.**

Strawberries Jamaica

1 (3-ounce) package cream cheese, softened
½ cup firmly packed brown sugar
1½ cups sour cream
1 to 2 tablespoons Grand Marnier or orange juice
Fresh strawberries

Beat cream cheese at medium speed of an electric mixer until smooth. Add brown sugar, sour cream, and Grand Marnier, stirring until blended. Cover and chill 8 hours. Serve with strawberries. **Yield: 2 cups.**

Honey-Gingered Pork Tenderloin

Pork Piccata

2 (¾-pound) pork tenderloins
½ cup all-purpose flour
½ teaspoon salt
¼ teaspoon pepper
3 tablespoons olive oil
½ cup Chablis or other dry white wine
½ cup lemon juice
3 tablespoons butter or margarine
¼ cup chopped fresh parsley
1½ tablespoons capers
Hot cooked fettuccine
Garnishes: lemon slices, fresh parsley sprigs

Cut each tenderloin into 6 (2-ounce) medaillons. Place, cut side down, between 2 sheets of heavy-duty plastic wrap; flatten to ¼-inch thickness, using a meat mallet or rolling pin.

Combine flour, salt, and pepper; dredge pork in flour mixture.

Cook half of pork in 1½ tablespoons olive oil in a large skillet over medium heat about 2 minutes on each side or until lightly browned. Remove from skillet; keep warm. Repeat procedure.

Add wine and lemon juice to skillet; cook until thoroughly heated. Add butter, chopped parsley, and capers, stirring until butter melts.

Arrange pork over pasta; drizzle with wine mixture. Garnish, if desired. Serve immediately. **Yield: 6 servings.**

Pork Piccata

Quick Summer Italian Salad

15 small fresh mushrooms
1 large cucumber, unpeeled and sliced
1 large green pepper, cut into strips
2 medium tomatoes, cut into wedges
½ cup chopped green onions
1 cup commercial Italian salad dressing
Lettuce leaves

Clean mushrooms with damp paper towels. Remove stems, and reserve for another use. Combine mushroom caps and next 5 ingredients in a large bowl; toss gently. Cover and chill. Serve on lettuce leaves. **Yield: 6 servings.**

Special Occasion Luncheon
(pictured on page 2)
SERVES 6
Lemon-Dill Chicken Sauté • Marinated Salad
French bread • Peachy Sherbet Cooler

Lemon-Dill Chicken Sauté

½ cup dry breadcrumbs
1½ teaspoons lemon-pepper seasoning
½ teaspoon dried dillweed
6 skinned and boned chicken breast halves
1 large egg, beaten
2 tablespoons vegetable oil

Combine first 3 ingredients in a dish. Dip chicken in egg; dredge in breadcrumb mixture.

Heat oil in a large skillet over medium heat. Add chicken, and cook 5 minutes on each side or until golden. Cover and cook 5 minutes. **Yield: 6 servings.**

TimeSavers

• For easy cleanup, use a plastic bag to dredge chicken.
• Layer salad in a glass bowl for a showy presentation; chill 8 hours.
• Get a headstart on dessert by peeling and halving peaches. Place in a bowl, and cover with pineapple juice to prevent discoloration. Drain before serving.

Marinated Salad

1 (15-ounce) can white asparagus spears, drained
1 (14-ounce) can artichoke hearts, drained and cut in half
1 (14-ounce) can hearts of palm, drained and cut into ½-inch slices
1 (4-ounce) can sliced mushrooms, drained
¼ cup sliced ripe olives
¼ cup sliced pimiento-stuffed olives
12 cherry tomatoes, halved
½ purple onion, sliced and separated into rings
1 (8-ounce) bottle Italian salad dressing
Romaine lettuce

Combine all ingredients except romaine lettuce in a bowl, stirring gently. Chill at least 30 minutes. Drain salad, and serve on lettuce. **Yield: 6 servings.**

Peachy Sherbet Cooler

3 peaches, peeled and halved
1 pint lime sherbet
1½ cups fresh raspberries
2 tablespoons peach schnapps

Place peach halves in individual serving dishes; top with a scoop of sherbet. Sprinkle with raspberries. Spoon 1 teaspoon peach schnapps over sherbet. Serve immediately. **Yield: 6 servings.**

Chicken-and-Rice Dinner

SERVES 4

Mediterranean Chicken • Hot cooked rice • Red Cabbage-Citrus Salad
Baked Ranch Tomatoes • Frozen yogurt • White wine

Mediterranean Chicken

4 skinned and boned chicken breast halves
3 tablespoons all-purpose flour
2 tablespoons olive oil
1 (14½-ounce) can ready-to-serve chicken broth
¼ cup sliced ripe olives
2 tablespoons capers
⅛ teaspoon pepper
1 (14-ounce) can whole artichoke hearts, rinsed and halved

Dredge chicken in flour; set aside.

Heat oil in a large skillet over medium-high heat. Add chicken, and cook 3 minutes on each side or until lightly browned.

Add chicken broth and next 3 ingredients. Bring to a boil; reduce heat, and simmer 15 minutes or until thickened and bubbly.

Stir in artichoke halves, and cook until mixture is thoroughly heated. **Yield: 4 servings.**

TimeSavers

- Dredge chicken in a plastic bag for easy cleanup.
- Cut salad preparation time by buying shredded cabbage and refrigerated orange sections.
- Cut a thin slice off the bottom of tomatoes to help them sit flat on the plate.

Red Cabbage-Citrus Salad

2 cups shredded red cabbage
4 large oranges, peeled and sectioned
½ cup coarsely chopped pecans, toasted
¼ cup chopped green onions
Commercial poppy seed dressing or sweet-and-sour salad dressing

Arrange cabbage evenly on individual salad plates; place orange sections in center. Sprinkle with pecans and green onions. Serve with dressing. **Yield: 4 to 6 servings.**

Baked Ranch Tomatoes

2 tomatoes, cut in half
Vegetable cooking spray
¼ teaspoon dried Italian seasoning
1½ tablespoons commercial Ranch-style dressing
Garnish: fresh parsley sprigs

Place tomato halves in an 8-inch square pan. Coat top of halves with cooking spray.

Bake tomato halves at 350° for 15 minutes.

Sprinkle with Italian seasoning, and top evenly with dressing.

Broil 3 inches from heat (with electric oven door partially opened) 2 to 3 minutes or until tomato halves begin to brown. Garnish, if desired. **Yield: 4 servings.**

Mediterranean Chicken

Summer Celebration

(pictured on page 117)

SERVES 8

Baked Chicken with Tarragon Sauce • Marinated Squash Medley
Crusty rolls • Coffee Crunch Parfaits • Iced tea

Baked Chicken with Tarragon Sauce

8 skinned and boned chicken breast halves
½ teaspoon salt
¼ teaspoon pepper
3 tablespoons lemon juice
½ cup mayonnaise or salad dressing
1 cup finely chopped celery
1 teaspoon dried tarragon
1 pound trimmed fresh spinach
3 medium tomatoes, cut into wedges
Garnish: celery leaves

Sprinkle chicken with salt and pepper. Arrange chicken in a lightly greased 13- x 9- x 2-inch pan; sprinkle with lemon juice.

Bake at 375° for 20 minutes or until tender. Chill 1 hour.

Combine mayonnaise, celery, and tarragon; set mixture aside.

Wash spinach, and pat dry. Arrange spinach on individual plates. Arrange chicken and tomato wedges over spinach. Spoon mayonnaise mixture over chicken. Garnish, if desired. **Yield: 8 servings.**

Note: For chicken salad, cooked chicken may be coarsely chopped and combined with mayonnaise mixture.

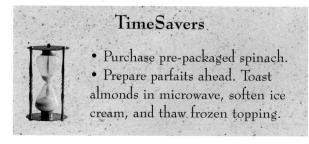

TimeSavers

• Purchase pre-packaged spinach.
• Prepare parfaits ahead. Toast almonds in microwave, soften ice cream, and thaw frozen topping.

Marinated Squash Medley

¾ cup olive oil
⅓ cup tarragon-flavored wine vinegar
2 tablespoons finely chopped shallots
1 clove garlic, minced
½ teaspoon salt
¼ teaspoon pepper
¼ teaspoon dried thyme
3 medium-size yellow squash, sliced
3 medium zucchini, sliced

Combine first 7 ingredients in a jar. Cover tightly, and shake vigorously.

Pour dressing over squash; toss gently. Cover and chill 4 hours. **Yield: 8 servings.**

Coffee Crunch Parfaits

1 quart coffee ice cream, softened
1 (2-ounce) package slivered almonds, chopped and toasted
2 (1⅛-ounce) English toffee-flavored candy bars, crushed
½ cup chocolate syrup
1 cup frozen whipped topping, thawed

Spoon ¼ cup ice cream into each of 8 (4-ounce) parfait glasses; freeze 15 minutes or until firm.

Layer half each of chopped almonds, crushed candy bars, and chocolate syrup evenly into glasses. Repeat layers with remaining ice cream, almonds, candy bars, and chocolate syrup.

Cover and freeze until firm. Top parfaits with whipped topping. **Yield: 8 parfaits.**

Saturday Night Buffet

SERVES 4 TO 6
Lime-Buttered Turkey Tenderloins • Asparagus-Carrot-Squash Toss
Almond Rice • Hot fudge sundaes

Lime-Buttered Turkey Tenderloins

¼ cup butter or margarine, melted
¼ cup lime juice
2 teaspoons dry mustard
2 teaspoons garlic salt
2 (¾-pound) turkey breast tenderloins
Garnishes: lime wedges, fresh parsley

Combine first 4 ingredients; divide in half.

Grill turkey, covered with grill lid, over medium-hot coals (350° to 400°) 4 to 5 minutes on each side or until meat thermometer registers 170°, turning once and basting often with half of marinade.

Cook remaining marinade in a small saucepan until thoroughly heated; serve warm with sliced turkey. Garnish, if desired. **Yield: 4 to 6 servings.**

Lime-Buttered Turkey Tenderloins

Asparagus-Carrot-Squash Toss

½ pound asparagus, cut into 1-inch pieces
½ pound carrots, cut into very thin strips
1 yellow squash, sliced
3 tablespoons butter or margarine, melted
3 tablespoons lemon juice
1 tablespoon chopped fresh dill or 1 teaspoon dried dillweed
¼ teaspoon salt

Combine vegetables, and place in a steamer rack over boiling water in a Dutch oven. Steam 8 to 10 minutes or until vegetables are crisp-tender.

Combine butter and remaining ingredients, and toss gently with vegetables. Serve immediately. **Yield: 4 to 6 servings.**

Almond Rice

1 (10½-ounce) can chicken broth, undiluted
1¼ cups water
1 cup long-grain rice, uncooked
½ cup slivered almonds
2 tablespoons butter or margarine, melted

Combine broth and water in a heavy saucepan; bring to a boil, and add rice. Cover, reduce heat, and simmer 20 minutes or until liquid is absorbed.

Cook almonds in butter in a skillet until lightly browned; stir into rice. **Yield: 4 to 6 servings.**

Grouper with Sautéed Vegetables

Fast Fish Feast

SERVES 4
Grouper with Sautéed Vegetables • Parmesan Noodles
Lettuce Wedges with Pimiento Dressing • Pineapple sherbet

Grouper with Sautéed Vegetables

1 small onion, thinly sliced
1 small green pepper, cut into strips
1 tablespoon olive oil
1 teaspoon garlic salt, divided
¾ teaspoon dried thyme, divided
1 medium tomato, peeled, seeded, and
　　chopped
1 (1-pound) grouper fillet
3 tablespoons lemon juice
¼ teaspoon hot sauce
Garnishes: leaf lettuce, lemon wedges

Combine first 3 ingredients in a 9-inch pieplate; sprinkle with ½ teaspoon garlic salt and ¼ teaspoon thyme. Microwave, uncovered, at HIGH 2 to 3 minutes. Stir in chopped tomato; microwave at HIGH 1 minute.

Cut fillet into 4 equal portions, and arrange in an 8-inch square baking dish, with thickest portions of fish toward outside of dish.

Combine lemon juice, hot sauce, remaining ½ teaspoon garlic salt, and ½ teaspoon thyme in a small bowl; pour over fish. Cover with wax paper, and microwave at HIGH 6 to 7 minutes or until fish flakes easily when tested with a fork. Drain.

Spoon vegetable mixture over fish; microwave at MEDIUM-HIGH (70% power) 1 minute. Garnish, if desired. **Yield: 4 servings.**

Parmesan Noodles

1 (8-ounce) package medium egg noodles
3 tablespoons butter or margarine, melted
⅛ teaspoon garlic powder
2 tablespoons chopped fresh parsley
2 tablespoons grated Parmesan cheese

Cook noodles according to package directions; drain well.

Toss noodles with butter, garlic powder, and parsley. Spoon into a serving bowl, and sprinkle with Parmesan cheese. Serve immediately. **Yield: 4 servings.**

Lettuce Wedges with Pimiento Dressing

3 tablespoons olive or vegetable oil
3 tablespoons red wine vinegar
1 tablespoon diced pimiento
1 teaspoon sugar
¼ teaspoon salt
¼ teaspoon pepper
1 medium head Boston lettuce, quartered

Combine first 6 ingredients in a jar. Cover tightly, and shake vigorously. Serve dressing over lettuce quarters. **Yield: 4 servings.**

TimeSavers

- Buy precut vegetables at a salad bar if you don't have a chopped supply in refrigerator.
- Make salad dressing the night before to allow flavors to blend.

Grilled Salmon Steaks

A Summer Delight

SERVES 4

Grilled Salmon Steaks • Sautéed zucchini strips ◆ Tomato-Feta Salad
Crusty rolls • ◆ Double-Delight Ice Cream Pie

Grilled Salmon Steaks

¼ cup mayonnaise
1 teaspoon chopped fresh dill or ¼ teaspoon
   dried dillweed
4 (1-inch-thick) salmon steaks
Garnishes: lemon halves, fresh dill sprigs

Combine mayonnaise and dill; spread on both sides of salmon.

Cook salmon, covered with grill lid, over medium-hot coals (350° to 400°) 5 to 6 minutes on each side or until done. Garnish, if desired. **Yield: 4 servings.**

Tomato-Feta Salad

¾ cup crumbled feta cheese
¼ cup chopped green onions
¾ teaspoon vegetable oil
½ teaspoon dried oregano
3 medium tomatoes, cut into wedges
Boston lettuce leaves

Combine first 5 ingredients; toss gently. Cover and chill at least 2 hours. Spoon onto Boston lettuce leaves to serve. **Yield: 4 servings.**

Double-Delight Ice Cream Pie

1½ cups butter pecan ice cream, softened
1 (9-inch) frozen graham cracker crust
2 (1⅛-ounce) English toffee-flavored candy
   bars, crushed
1½ cups vanilla ice cream, softened

Spread butter pecan ice cream in graham cracker crust. Sprinkle with half of crushed candy bars; freeze. Spread vanilla ice cream over top, and sprinkle with remaining crushed candy bars; freeze until firm. **Yield: one 9-inch pie.**

TimeSavers

• Preheat gas grill 20 minutes or light charcoal fire 30 minutes ahead.
• Save time and nutrients by not peeling the tomatoes.
• Make pie ahead; soften solidly frozen ice cream by microwaving at HIGH 10 seconds or until soft.

Elegant Tuna Dinner

SERVES 4

Tuna Steaks with Tarragon Butter
Buttered orzo and parsley • Vegetable Sauté • Sourdough Wedges
Angel food cake and strawberries

Tuna Steaks with Tarragon Butter

¼ cup butter or margarine, softened
½ teaspoon lemon juice
1 teaspoon minced fresh tarragon or ½
    teaspoon dried tarragon
4 (½-pound) tuna steaks (about ¾ inch thick)
½ teaspoon salt
½ teaspoon freshly ground pepper
2 tablespoons olive oil

Combine first 3 ingredients; shape into a 1-inch-thick log; cover and chill until firm.

Sprinkle tuna with salt and pepper on all sides. Heat olive oil in a nonstick skillet over medium heat; cook tuna 5 minutes on each side or until desired degree of doneness. Slice tarragon butter, and serve with tuna. **Yield: 4 servings.**

Vegetable Sauté

2 tablespoons olive oil
1 large zucchini, sliced
1 large yellow squash, sliced
1 carrot, scraped and sliced
1 clove garlic, crushed
½ teaspoon pepper
¼ teaspoon hot sauce

Heat olive oil in a large skillet until hot; add remaining ingredients, and toss gently. Cover, reduce heat, and cook 10 minutes or until crisp-tender. **Yield: 4 servings.**

Sourdough Wedges

4 (2-ounce) sourdough rolls, cut into quarters
Butter-flavored cooking spray
1 tablespoon grated Parmesan cheese
¼ teaspoon paprika

Coat cut surfaces of rolls with cooking spray. Combine Parmesan cheese and paprika; sprinkle mixture on cut surfaces, and place bread on a baking sheet.

Broil 6 inches from heat (with electric oven door partially opened) 2 to 3 minutes or until rolls are golden. **Yield: 4 servings.**

TimeSavers

• If desired, substitute rice for orzo, a rice-shaped pasta which cooks quickly.
• Shape and chill tarragon butter in advance, or, if short on time, dollop tarragon butter on tuna steaks.
• Purchase angel food cake from the bakery of your local supermarket, or make one from a mix. Serve with fresh strawberries or other fruits in season.

Tuna Steaks with Tarragon Butter

Easy Crab Imperial

Imperial Dinner
SERVES 4
Easy Crab Imperial • Minted Peas and Peppers • Sliced tomatoes
Sesame rolls • Mocha Polka

Easy Crab Imperial

1 pound fresh lump crabmeat, drained
⅔ cup mayonnaise or salad dressing
1 tablespoon chopped fresh parsley
2 teaspoons lemon juice
3 to 4 tablespoons grated Parmesan cheese
Paprika

Combine first 4 ingredients. Spoon about ½ cup mixture into 4 shell-shaped baking dishes; sprinkle with cheese. Bake at 350° for 15 minutes or until thoroughly heated. Sprinkle with paprika. **Yield: 4 servings.**

Minted Peas and Peppers

½ pound fresh snow pea pods
1 tablespoon butter or margarine
1 large sweet red pepper, cut into ¼-inch
  strips
2 tablespoons chopped onion
1 teaspoon chopped fresh mint
¼ teaspoon salt

Wash snow peas; trim ends, and remove any tough strings. Set aside.

Place butter in a shallow 1½-quart casserole; microwave at HIGH 35 seconds or until melted. Add snow peas, red pepper, and remaining ingredients.

Cover tightly with heavy-duty plastic wrap; fold back a small corner of wrap to allow steam to escape. Microwave at HIGH 4 minutes or until vegetables are crisp-tender, stirring after 2 minutes. Serve immediately. **Yield: 4 servings.**

Mocha Polka

1 pint chocolate ice cream
2 cups cold coffee
1 tablespoon rum
Whipped cream
Ground nutmeg

Combine first 3 ingredients in container of an electric blender; process until smooth. Pour into glasses, and top with whipped cream. Sprinkle with nutmeg, and serve immediately. **Yield: 4 cups.**

TimeSavers

• Easy Crab Imperial may be baked in 4 baked (3-inch) pastry shells.
• Substitute frozen snow peas for fresh ones.
• Halve and seed red pepper; then place, skin side down, on cutting board and slice. It is easier to slice a pepper if cut from the flesh (not the skin) side.

Festive Shrimp Supper

SERVES 6

Shrimp Scampi • ◆ Marinated Asparagus and Hearts of Palm
French bread • ◆ Easy Individual Trifles • White wine

Shrimp Scampi

1 medium onion, finely chopped
4 cloves garlic, minced
½ cup butter or margarine, melted
½ teaspoon dried tarragon
2 tablespoons fresh lemon juice
½ teaspoon steak sauce
½ teaspoon Worcestershire sauce
¼ teaspoon hot sauce
2 pounds peeled, jumbo fresh shrimp
2 tablespoons chopped fresh parsley
Hot cooked fettuccine

Cook onion and garlic in butter in a large skillet over medium heat, stirring constantly, 3 to 4 minutes; add tarragon and next 4 ingredients. Bring to a boil; add shrimp, and cook, stirring constantly, 5 to 6 minutes or until shrimp turn pink. Sprinkle with parsley. Serve over fettuccine. **Yield: 6 servings.**

Marinated Asparagus and Hearts of Palm

1½ pounds fresh asparagus
1 (14-ounce) can hearts of palm, drained and
     cut into ½-inch slices
½ cup vegetable oil
¼ cup cider vinegar
1 clove garlic, crushed
¾ teaspoon salt
½ teaspoon pepper
Cherry tomatoes

Snap off tough ends of asparagus. Place asparagus in steaming rack over boiling water; cover and steam 4 minutes. Drain and submerge in ice water to cool. Drain asparagus well.

Combine asparagus and hearts of palm in a heavy-duty, zip-top plastic bag. Combine oil and next 4 ingredients in a jar; cover and shake vigorously. Pour over vegetables. Seal bag, and marinate in refrigerator 8 hours; turn bag occasionally. Add tomatoes. **Yield: 6 servings.**

Easy Individual Trifles

1 (3-ounce) package ladyfingers
¼ cup seedless raspberry jam
2 tablespoons dry sherry
2 tablespoons orange juice
2 cups milk
1 (3.4-ounce) package vanilla instant pudding
     mix
1 (8.5-ounce) can refrigerated instant whipped
     cream
2 tablespoons slivered almonds, toasted

Halve ladyfingers lengthwise. Spread 1 teaspoon jam on bottom half of each ladyfinger; cover each with top, and cut in half crosswise.

Arrange 4 filled halves in each individual serving dish; drizzle each with 1 teaspoon sherry and 1 teaspoon orange juice.

Combine milk and pudding mix in a 1-quart container; cover tightly, and shake 45 seconds. Pour over ladyfingers.

Chill at least 4 hours. Just before serving, top with whipped cream and almonds. **Yield: 6 servings.**

Shrimp Scampi

Fiery Cajun Feast

SERVES 6 TO 8
Fiery Cajun Shrimp • Corn on the Cob
◆ Green salad with Vinaigrette Dressing • French bread
Watermelon slices

Fiery Cajun Shrimp

1 cup butter, melted
1 cup margarine, melted
½ cup Worcestershire sauce
¼ cup lemon juice
¼ cup ground pepper
2 teaspoons hot sauce
2 teaspoons salt
4 cloves garlic, minced
5 pounds unpeeled, medium-size fresh shrimp
2 lemons, thinly sliced
French bread

   Combine first 8 ingredients; pour half of mixture into a large ceramic heat-proof dish. Layer shrimp and lemon slices in sauce; pour remaining sauce over shrimp and lemon.
   Bake, uncovered, at 400° for 20 minutes or until shrimp turn pink, stirring twice. Drain sauce, and serve with shrimp and French bread. **Yield: 6 to 8 servings.**

Fiery Cajun Shrimp

Vinaigrette Dressing

¼ cup white wine vinegar
1 teaspoon lemon juice
⅛ teaspoon garlic powder or 1 clove garlic, minced
½ teaspoon Dijon mustard
⅛ teaspoon salt
½ cup olive oil

   Combine first 5 ingredients; slowly add olive oil, stirring constantly with a wire whisk until blended. Serve over green salad. **Yield: ¾ cup.**

TimeSavers

• Melt butter and margarine in a 4-cup glass measure in microwave.
• Make Vinaigrette Dressing ahead. Mince enough garlic and squeeze lemon juice for dressing and shrimp.

Index